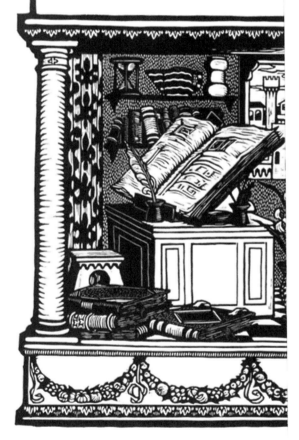

The Venerable Tibetan Mastiff

by Max Siber

revised and edited by Cathy J. Flamholtz

Classic Dog Book Series

OTR Publications

ISBN 0-940269-09-0

Library of Congress Cataloging-in-Publication Data

Siber, Max
    [Tibethund. English]
    The venerable Tibetan Mastiff / by Max Siber: revised and
edited by Cathy J. Flamholtz.
       p. cm. — (Classic dog book series)
    Includes bibliographical references (p.   ).
    ISBN 0-940269-09-0
    1. Tibetan mastiff.   I. Flamholtz, Cathy J.   II. Title.
III. Series.
SF429.T48S5313   1995
636.7 '3--dc20   95-37185
                                         CIP

Printed in the United States of America

10 9 8 7 6 5 4 3 2 1

Although the authors have extensively researched sources to ensure the accuracy and completeness of the information contained in this book, we assume no responsibility for errors, inaccuracies, omissions or any inconsistency herein. Any slights of people or organizations are unintentional.

OTR PUBLICATIONS
P.O. Box 481
Centreville, AL 35042

4

Dedication

To my close friend Ann Rohrer,

whose commitment, love for the breed and hard
work did so much to launch the Tibetan Mastiff
in the United States

Originally published as

Der Tibethund

by Chief Forester

Max Siber

Winterthür, Switzerland

in the year 1897

Original Dedication

Dedicated in closest friendship

to

Animal Artist Richard Strebel

of

Munich, Germany

Contents

Introduction

by

Cathy J. Flamholtz

"In the foreseeable, if not immediate, future we shall find the Tibet Mastiff at all of our dog shows. It will take only a few generations to make a watch-dog, companion dog and impressive luxury-dog out of him, at least in the majority of the specimens bred, which would be suited to and fit for our western civilization."

These words were penned by Swiss dog writer Max Siber in 1897. He would, doubtless, be astounded to learn that it was not until the 1970s that the Tibetan Mastiff would finally gain a lasting foothold in the western dog world.

Siber lived in one of the most exciting periods in western dogdom. In England, such legendary names as Drury and Idstone were taking pen in hand to explore the origins and histories of our dog breeds. Shaw and Stonehenge were busy working on their later books. In Belgium, Count Henri de Bylandt was writing his famed dog classic. In France, Pierre Mégnin and Adolph Reul were sharing their opinions with eager readers while, in

Germany, such legendaries as Richard Strebel and Ludwig Beckmann were recording their insights into canine history. Theories, thoughts, opinions and hypotheses abounded during this period.

Siber was himself a respected member of the European dog world. Switzerland held its first dog show in 1871 and published the first stud book in 1884. Swiss breeders had begun to take an interest in their native breed, the Saint Bernard. Max Siber, a respected Saint breeder, edited many of the early Swiss Canine Society Stud Books. Under his guidance, these books became a forum for some of the most innovative Swiss and German thinkers of the day. In 1893, he judged at a Zurich show, where he was presented with an entry of 99 Saints.

In the 1880s, Siber had made several expeditions to learn more about dogs. We do not know exactly where his travels took him. However, his discovery, in Sumatra, of the previously unknown Battak-Spitz added greatly to the knowledge of dogs and their place in primitive societies. Capt. von Stephanitz, the father of the modern German Shepherd, quoted Siber's report on the Battak-Spitz extensively in his classic *The German Shepherd Dog in Word and Picture*. It's also likely that Siber journeyed to Africa, recording his findings in the rare book, *Dogs of Africa*.

Siber was always fascinated by the Tibetan Mastiff. It tantalized him because the great dog of

Tibet was consistently mentioned as the grand-daddy, the Adam, of most of the existing breeds of large dogs. He eagerly read accounts, from Aristotle to the reports of 19th century archae-ologists, in an attempt to learn all he could about the breed. He pored through travel books, culling information as he went. He spoke with those whose expeditions had taken them to the Roof of the World.

Finally, in 1888, he made his own pilgrim-age. He traveled to British India in an attempt to finally see Tibetan Mastiffs in their native habi-tat. It must have been a terrible blow when he found no dogs and learned that the people he questioned knew little about them. Still, he plod-ded on. He made his way to the Himalayan foot-hills and discovered a few dogs. He spoke with Tibetans who told him about the large dogs found in their homeland. His dream, though, of finding large numbers of purebred dogs, such as the ones he had envisioned, was dashed.

Thankfully, for us, he was still enthralled by the breed. With the support and encourage-ment of friends, such as the renowned German writer Richard Strebel, he decided to write a book, sharing with fellow dog fanciers all he had learned of this ancient breed. It was published in 1897, with the title *Der Tibethund.*

That a book on an unknown breed should have been published, at that early date, is really quite amazing. In England, very few individual breed books had been published prior to 1897. Those few were mainly limited to the most popular breeds: Foxhounds, Fox Terriers, Greyhounds, Irish Wolfhounds and Mastiffs. At the time Siber penned his text, only a handful of Tibetan Mastiffs had made their way to the western world. There were no established breeders, no breed club and no sign that there would soon be sufficient stock to merit such a book. We all know what current publishers would say if approached with a proposal for a book on a poorly represented breed.

When my friend Ann Rohrer and I were writing *The Tibetan Mastiff, Legendary Guardian of the Himalayas,* in 1989, we would occasionally come across references to *Der Tibethund.* I became intrigued by the idea of a book on the breed published at such an early date. Yet, no one seemed to have a copy of it. A couple of years ago, successful TM breeder Karen Pickel and her husband were transferred to Germany. There, Karen was fortunate enough to obtain a photocopy of *Der Tibethund,* which was relayed to Ann and then to me. How tantalizing to have a copy of this scarce book in my hands and yet how frustrating to be unable to read it in German. Finally, I arranged for a translation. I believed that TM fanciers would benefit from reading Siber's work and this is now offered in *The Venerable Tibetan Mastiff.*

Special thanks go to Karen Pickel and Ann Rohrer for providing me with a copy of this book. Enormous thanks are due German fancier Bill Ledbetter for his help in preparing the manuscript. My deep appreciation goes, also, to OTR Publications for agreeing to publish *The Venerable Tibetan Mastiff.*

The Venerable Tibetan Mastiff offers Tibetan Mastiff fanciers a valuable new source of information on the breed. Due to the language barrier, our present knowledge has been confined to books printed in English. Max Siber's work throws open the door to new sources. Here we find the opinions of the foremost German, Swiss and French authorities of the time.

It is amazing to me, as I am sure it will be to many of you, that some of the subjects Siber discusses are still being debated today. Scholars, in the 1890s, argued about the proper categorization of the breed. Should the TM be classified as a "mastiff" or a "mountain dog"? What is the proper size for the breed? Does size vary depending on the region of origin? All of these questions bedeviled Siber and his colleagues, just as they do present-day breeders.

I hope that readers will delight in *The Venerable Tibetan Mastiff.* Finally, just shy of 100 years after he wrote this work, Max Siber can be appreciated for his contribution to the breed.

Editor's Note

by

Cathy J. Flamholtz

When working on a book like this one, there are always judgment calls. Should an attempt be made to modernize the text or do we follow the original closely, even though parts of it are obsolete? I have chosen, whenever possible, to preserve the original for its historical significance. Therefore, modern readers are apt to find Siber's writing style a little stilted and, inevitably, some of his opinions outdated. Rather than editing out these viewpoints, I chose to include them, feeling that they reflect the thinking of his time and would be of interest to today's readers. I have, on occasion, supplemented the text with a few clearly marked footnotes of my own.

In the main, Siber uses the appellation "Tibet Mastiff" to describe the breed. I have let this stand rather than converting the references to the more commonly accepted "Tibetan Mastiff."

I have also taken the liberty of reorganizing Siber's work, creating logical chapter breaks in place of the single monograph that he presented. This, I felt, would make the text more suitable to today's readers.

The greatest challenge, by far, was dealing with the photos and illustrations contained in the original book. In many cases, Siber substituted drawings for photographs that were not available to him. This was particularly true with bas-reliefs and sculptures discovered by archaeologists. I have sought out photographs of the originals, upon which the drawings were based, and included those instead. Since I was forced to use a photocopy of Siber's original publication, some of Siber's photographs were simply unsuitable for reproduction. It's impossible to say how good the appearance of the original photos were, as the quality of illustrations in many books from the 1800s is simply not up to current publishing standards. Where necessary, I have taken the liberty of substituting other photos and/or drawings which illustrate Siber's points. It was also apparent that Siber was extremely limited in the number of Tibetan Mastiff depictions that were available for inclusion in the original work. A number of photographs of Great Danes, Saint Bernards and Newfoundlands were featured in *Der Tibethund.* I had a much greater choice of photographic material available and was able to include many more drawings of Tibetan Mastiffs. I have tried, to the best of my ability, to remain faithful to the original book. On several occasions, I felt that there was merit in including the original drawing or photo, even though I knew that the reproduction quality would be poor. Through the use of computer enhancement, OTR has made every effort to make these illustrations as clear as possible. I apologize, though, for the grainy nature and lack of clarity in these photos.

Der *Tibethund* included 40 illustrations. I have chosen to add to this number by including other depictions of Tibetan Mastiffs that were not available to Siber. I hope that these changes will make the book more enjoyable for everyone.

Cathy J. Flamholtz
July 1995

"Sunt qui Seras alunt, genus intractabilis
    irae."

(Gratius Valiacus: Carmen Venaucum
    159 A.D.)

Translation from the Latin:

"Furthermore, the dogs which the Tibetans
(Serers) raise and breed are known: a wayward, headstrong, unruly breed, which is
famous for its savage ferocity."

"Tibet is the most wretched country in the
world; it is unique, however, in producing
both the most beautiful girls and women and
the most vicious, ill-tempered dogs."

(Chinese opinion with regard to
Tibet, as published in Kreitner, 1855)

"Carnivora," a rare 1880 colored print, by Henry J. Johnson, showing the Tibetan Mastiff. *From the Flamholtz collection.*

Chapter One

The Tibetan Mastiff: Mastiff or Mountain Dog?

With the following study we shall strive to give our readers as complete a picture as possible of the Tibet Mastiff, with which we had the opportunity of becoming acquainted near his original ancestral homeland. We shall represent exactly almost all the details that are known about this unique breed, even if these details are repetitive. It has been proven that this extremely interesting type of dog has existed for 2,500-3,000 years without undergoing any anatomical changes whatsoever in its present-day native homeland: mountainous highlands of extreme altitude, which have been completely isolated from the rest of the world since time immemorial, as far as we know from our studies in ancient history.

The two most immense, vast mountain-chains in the Old World, with the most snow and glaciers, the Alps and the Himalayas, quarter two of the largest, most unique dog breeds: the St. Bernard (Alps) and the Tibet Mastiff (Himalayas). In spite of the extreme geographic separation of their native homelands, these two breeds show many similar characteristics. Both breeds are representatives of the same group of large Molossus-type dogs, all of which have broad foreheads and short muzzles, great height at the withers, with huge overall size, heavy bone-structure and broad, high-set flop-ears. Belonging to this same group of dogs are: the Old German Bear-Biters, the Old Bull-Biters of the Middle Ages, the primeval War or Military Dogs of central Europe, the Dogue de Bordeaux, the Mastiff breeds and the extremely large Spanish Mastin.[1]

One must not confuse this group of *genuine* Molossus dogs with the present-day Great Dane, which was obviously produced by blending sighthounds (for example, smooth-coated Greyhounds) or lighter-boned Pariah-dog forms with the genuine, massive, broad-foreheaded Molossus dog. Those of my readers who wish to thoroughly inform themselves with regard to these questions should read the chapter about the Molossus group in Beckmann's standard book on dog breeds entitled *Die Hunderassen (The Dog Breeds)*. In this regard, Beckmann and we share, independently of each other, the same opinion. It is therefore not completely incorrect when all the English dog-book authors since Buffon name our present-day German Molossus-like dog "the Great Dane" and do not call him the "German Mastiff"; or when

Drawing of the impressive St. Bernard Champion Sir Bedivere, by celebrated animal artist G. Muss-Arnolt. *From the Flamholtz collection.*

the Italians call him the "Grand Danese" instead of "Molosso" or "Alano"; or when the French call him the "Grand Danois" instead of "Dogue Allemand" (German Mastiff). The Great Dane that we now have is simply not a *genuine* Molossus-type dog from a scientific point of view, but only a partial derivative thereof.

The transitional form between the old Molossus type and the modern form of the Great Dane could possibly best be represented by the large "Danish" dog. The extremely bulky, coarse head with pronounced cheeks is a remnant of the "old type" Great Dane; the body anatomy and

Turn of the century Great Danes. From *Kennel Secrets*, by Ashmont.

overall form, however, is representative of the "new type".

It has been observed that, universally, all high-mountain regions of the Old World possess, without exception, particularly large types of dogs, all distinguished by great strength, power and courage, and frequently also by their ferocity. We only must recall the gigantic Shepherd dogs of Spain's Sierra d'Estrella, namely the Great Pyrenees; or Italy's dogs of the Apennines and the Abruzzi Mountains; or the huge, ferocious Shepherd dogs of the Balkan Peninsula, of Albania and of Greece; or the very large dogs of the Caucasus Mountains described by Radde; or the colossal and vicious breeds of the Kandahar region or of Afghanistan, etc.

Formerly it was thought that the above-mentioned dogs could all be placed together into the same group called "Mountain Dogs", along with the St. Bernard (from the Swiss Alps) and the Tibet Mastiff (from the highlands of Central Asia). This grouping, however, was probably incorrect. With regard to their skulls and overall anatomy, the St. Bernard and the Tibet Mastiff are strikingly different from the other mountain dogs of Europe and Asia. With regard to their skulls, they seem to have gradually evolved from a form of *Canis familiaris palustris* (the Stone Age Torfhund or Dog of the Peat Bogs),[2] while the other above-mentioned breeds, in comparison, are more "wolf-like" in type, not only with regard to their head form, but also in the form and setting of their eyes and in their overall external appearance. Those other breeds have far closer relationship to their progenitor, the wolf, than do the St. Bernard and Tibet Mastiff.[3]

From the prehistorical period, only a few skulls bearing relationship to the St. Bernard have been found by archaeologists here in Europe. In the old settlements of the Lake Dwellers, dating back to the Stone Age, skulls of this size have not been found here in Switzerland. On the other hand, Professor Nehring of Berlin was able to obtain very large skulls of domesticated dogs that had been found by German archaeologists: he named this large type of Stone Age dog *Canis familiaris decumanus*. Professor Theodor Studer of Bern, Switzerland, did recently obtain a very large, ancient skull found in Lake Constance (Konstanz, Bodensee, in southwest Germany). This skull, however, seems to be the missing link to the Deerhound rather than the connection to the St. Bernard. (Refer to Swiss Dog Registry, Vol. 5.)

It is remarkable, nevertheless, that the largest, most massive and powerful dogs on earth are found high up in the most immense mountain-chains of highest altitude. Such steep terrain is relatively infertile and, due to the extreme altitude, usually a bleak, dreary climate prevails. This would impede the reproduction of such huge dogs.

An early etching of a Tibetan Mastiff; artist unknown. *From Hutchinson's Dog Encyclopedia.*

One would think that in such mountain-chains, providing only the barest meager nutrition, only small, relatively frail dogs would be found—or at any rate, extremely agile, lightly-built dogs capable of scaling the steep terrain. Surprisingly, the opposite is true: the largest, most massive dogs in the world are found here. This also applies to several other species of domesticated animals found in mountainous regions. For example, here in Switzerland, our largest breed of cattle is found in the mountains of Tirol (in Austria and northern Italy): the Pinzgauer cattle breed. In the Himalayas we find, in the foothills, a very massive, large black-and-white variety of the Zebu (Brahma cattle), which in size resemble our Simmentalers and, in color, the black-and-white variety of Simmentalers bred in Freiburg, Germany. They are, in relationship to the cattle of the Bengali plains, like a French Percheron draught-horse compared to a slender, fine-boned Arabian horse of the desert. In the mountains of western Turkey we find the giant Bergamasker sheep, compared with which the North German moorland sheep appear to be a dwarf breed. In addition, we find this to be true among wild canids (wolf, coyote, jackal, fox). In the museum in Calcutta, India, there are several species of the wild-dog, belonging to the genus *Cuon*, displayed for comparison next to each other. The species from the hill regions and the plains, *Cuon primaevus*, *Cuon dukhunensis* and *Cuon rutilans*, are light in build, skittish, easily excitable animals. In build, they are similar to Greyhounds or other sight-hounds, perhaps even pariah-dogs. The *Cuon alpinus*, however, which lives in the high mountains of central Asia and Siberia, is significantly larger and heavier. As a matter of fact, it looks far more like a yellow, heavy-boned Leonberger than any breed, irrespective naturally of the characteristics which clearly separate the two groups of animals (*Cuon* and *Canis*): skull, muzzle-line, bite, etc.

It is to be assumed that in the mountains, where the hard struggle for existence prevailed over a very long period of time, a large, massive, strong, robust type of animal was developed. All weaker individuals were eliminated or displaced by means of natural selection; only the strongest, fittest, best-adapted individuals could survive and remain there in these mountainous regions, There these animals developed to become the massive, strong breeds of mountain animals found in the European Alps and the Himalayas.

Tibet Mastiffs and St. Bernards show, in spite of the thousands of kilometers separating them, many similarities. In spite of the interesting hypotheses[4] developed on the historical basis of mass migrations (of Stone Age man and later of the Aryans) westward from Asia to Europe, a direct genetic relationship of the Tibet Mastiff and St. Bernard is highly improbable.[5] We must, therefore assume that environmental, ecological and climatic factors within two different geographically isolated regions created simultaneously two different breeds with many similar characteristics.

Professor Theodor Studer of Bern, Switzerland, who is also famous for his intensive, long studies over the subject-areas dealing with the development of the domesticated dog, has recently published a very noteworthy article entitled "Contributions on the History of our Dog Breeds" (published in the Catalog of Group 45, Hunting Breeds, for the Dog Show in Geneva, Switzerland in 1896, and in the Swiss Dog Registry Book, Volume VII, 1897.)

An original drawing of a "Tibet Mastiff" by the famous Swiss artist Richard Strebel, to whom this book was originally dedicated. Note the yaks grazing in the background.

This article has contributed a lot toward finding an answer to the question as to why the Alps and Himalayas have such similar breeds. The answer to this question lies in the ancestry which both the Tibet Mastiff and St. Bernard have in common. The progenitors, from which both breeds developed and differentiated, are identical.

Professor Studer's conception of the development of our breeds is shown in the following table, the results of his scientifically conducted archaeological studies of fossil skulls and bones coincide almost exactly with our own conclusions drawn empirically through intensive observation

Richard Strebel later modified the drawing of the Tibet Mastiff pictured opposite. Note that this later depiction is much more realistic in presentation.

during our long journeys to and travel within remote regions of Europe and Asia.

The Palaearctic Dogs (of Europe and of Northern and Central Asia) were developed in the following manner:

I.) *Canis familiaris palustris* : (Stone Age *Torfspitz* of the Lake Dwellers)
  a.) all German and other Central European Spitz varieties
  b.) Dutch Keeshond = German Wolfsspitz
  c.) the Siberian Spitz varieties and Chow-Chow
  d.) the Battak-Dogs (Battak-Spitz of Sumatra)
  e.) Pinschers and Schnauzers

II.) *Canis familiaris Inostranzewi*
    a.) Russian Laikas
    b.) Arctic Eskimo sled-dogs
    c.) Mastiffs (including the *Tibet Mastiff)*
    d.) Great Danes
    e.) Molossus breeds
    f.) Laika sled-dogs
    g.) Newfoundland
    h.) St. Bernard

III.) *Canis familiaris Leineri*
    a.) Deerhounds
    b.) Irish Wolfhound

IV.) *Canis familiaris matris optimae*
    a.) Shepherds
    b.) Sheep-Dogs
    c.) Poodles

V.) *Canis familiaris intermedius* : (Hunting dog of
    the Bronze Age)
    a.) Scent Hounds
    b.) Bird Dogs (Pointers, Setters)
    c.) Spaniels
    d.) Silken Quail Dog (Seidenwachtelhund)

The Tibet Mastiff and the St. Bernard have the same Stone Age progenitor in Form II *(Canis familiaris Inostranzewi),* in which Professor Studer also groups the Russian Laika and the Siberian and

Arctic sled-dogs of the Eskimos. I would have also placed the Chinese Chow-Chow into this group. If we accept this hypothesis, it is clearly understood why these two mountain breeds, the Tibet Mastiff and the St. Bernard, have so many similarities.

I saw dogs in the foot-hills of the Himalayas which definitely had Tibet Mastiff ancestry from their appearance and their movement; and these dogs could just as easily have been whelped here in Switzerland. We still find Swiss dogs nowadays that a person would immediately classify as being dogs from India, if they had ever beforehand seen blends of the Tibet Mastiff, which are often found in the Himalayan foothills and plains of India. One

An 1896 drawing of Saint Bernards by Swiss artist Richard Strebel.

A Saint Bernard showing the so-called "partial" or "adaptive albinism" to which Siber refers.

must not forget, however, that the *true* Tibet Mastiff lives completely isolated in the Himalayas, and that the Mastiff-like dogs of India's Bengali plain or of the Punjab area are so *distantly* related to the true Tibet Mastiff that it is inconceivable that any kinship to our Swiss dogs could exist. There can only remain, therefore, the plain, bare fact that in two separate locations, isolated from each other and far apart, which, however, possess similar geographical, environmental and climatic conditions, two very similar breeds of the domesticated dog evolved. The objection could be raised: "What, indeed, are the similarities of the St. Bernard and the Tibet Mastiff? The Tibet Mastiff is black in color, the St. Bernard is often almost white. The St. Bernard has a shorter-coated hair length, the Tibet Mastiff is longer-coated,"—These contradictions are, at first glance, legitimate and not easily explained. Why is it that the Tibet Mastiff is dark-colored, although he comes in contact with snow just as often as the Swiss St. Bernard? St. Bernards tend to be somewhat albino as a result of adaptation to their snowy homeland.[6] They were bred to be whiter and whiter from generation to generation here in Switzerland's snow-covered mountains, while the St. Bernards bred in less snowy valley regions or in England, where much less snow falls, quickly regain dark patches and spotting. At the present time, we are unable to offer an adequate explanation for these contradictions.[7] We might add, however, that particularly this "partial or adaptive albinism" appeared as a product of intensive incest breeding, and that, in addition to this color variation, the colors deep-red, black and yellow spontaneously appear occasionally in St. Bernard breeding programs here in Switzerland; some are more Mastiff-like in build with broad foreheads, very similar in appearance to the Tibet Mastiff in such characteristics. The apparent contradiction with regard to coat-type could possibly be explained when we consider that the St. Bernard is found both in the long-coated and short-coated varieties; and we also know that there are many Tibet Mastiffs that are really long-coated only on certain body parts, while they usually otherwise have a rough coat of medium length, with a dense undercoat during the winter.[8]

Both breeds show correspondence in body anatomy, eye-form and eye-color, movement and even in the carriage of the tail while fulfilling their duties. In both breeds—of course, we are only speaking here of the outstanding representatives of the two breeds—the head is worthy of special notice on account of its size and form. The front part of the body is, in comparison with the rear portion, paramount. The head appears to be the most important part of the body. In both breeds, the hindquarters are somewhat less strongly developed than in some of the other larger breeds: the thigh region could be somewhat more muscular in most individuals; the hind legs have a tendency to be somewhat straight stifled or slightly cow-hocked, [which is a tendency found invariably even among wild animal species developed in mountainous regions, for example all forms of the wild mountain goat (ibex)

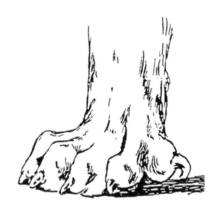

The foot of either a St. Bernard or a Tibetan Mastiff. The presence of the fifth and sixth toe should be observed—these are the so-called "double wolf claws," or "double dewclaws." The first toe is not visible here; it is on the left side.

and the chamois, both of which are extremely cow-hocked.] Both breeds have dewclaws, and frequently not only this fifth toe, but also a sixth toe on the hind feet[9]; in rare cases, the sixth toe can also be found on the front feet. Strangely enough, this peculiarity is also pronounced in other mountain breeds of dogs. In both breeds, the Tibet Mastiff and the St. Bernard, the lower eye-lid forms an angular fold or wrinkle. This eye-lid does not tightly enclose the eyeball, but sticks out slightly and reveals the red, bloodshot conjunctiva. Both breeds have broad, rather high set ears; both have similar gaits and occasionally rather unwieldy movement.

The two breeds perhaps differ most with regard to the form of their heads. The head of the Tibet Mastiff is longer, namely at the muzzle region, and narrower between the eyes; in addition, the Tibet Mastiff's upper skull is more arched, more closely resembling that of the Bloodhound, as the English dog breeders say, than that of the St. Bernard. These, however, are the differences found when comparing the extreme representatives of both breeds. The average Tibet Mastiff is not more remarkable with regard to a distinct head form than the average representatives of one of our other larger breeds. Conversely, we have, among our larger European breeds, representatives which clearly resemble the more outstanding Tibet Mastiffs with regard to head form. Nowadays, we would obviously have far more with this head type, had this characteristic been preferred and selected by the St. Bernard breeders.

In the 1860s, shortly after the English had first discovered the St. Bernard in Switzerland, many so-called St. Bernards were shown in England, which had been derived from early Swiss breeding stock. Some of these were black with tan (or yellowish) markings; and, as is documented in the English judges' evaluations, these dogs were Tibet-Mastiff-like. The most noted among these dogs was a black-and-tan St. Bernard male from Valais named "Menthon".

The long-haired St. Bernard "Chang." Note the resemblance to early TM type. Chang is a grandson of "Menthon," mentioned by Siber. Apparently his type was quite strong.

Chapter Two

Ancient History

With our still very limited knowledge concerning the country of Tibet nowadays, the dog breed developed in and typical of that bleak, mountainous region was, already in remote antiquity, known to the civilized lands of that ancient period.

That may in part result from the fact that he not only was present at that time already in Tibet itself, but also in central, and particularly in the far eastern Himalayas, in relatively pure breeding programs. Just so, he can be found nowadays in the regions of Bischur, Nepal, Bhutan, Junan and in the Chinese province of Kan-su, sometimes purebred, but frequently in more or less related variations of the pure form. We do *not* find him, however, in ancient Egypt. Among the numerous famous dog pictures from that region, his portrait is nowhere to be found. The presumption that he was not known there at all, at least not by name, is untenable, because he was found in Assyria already around the year 700 B.C. Probably he either did not survive the journey to Egypt through the deserts and across the extremely sunny, hot and humid Red Sea, or he rapidly died out in the new climate, so completely different from that to which he was adapted. We even now have reports that the Tibet Mastiff is very difficult to acclimatize in tropical regions or that he degenerates and ages too rapidly there. And only with great difficulty, can he endure the trip from his mountainous homeland, which nowadays is relatively quick, into regions with a moderate, warmer climate.

With regard to the manifest canine sport, in which the "Wonderland of the Pyramids" was already engaged in most ancient times, it cannot be assumed that his importation was not attempted. Even in pictures from the ancient Greek and Roman periods, the Tibet Mastiff, strangely enough, was not documented and preserved for us. Greek historians and writers mention him repeatedly and the Romans describe dogs which could scarcely have been anything other than derivatives of the Tibet Mastiff. Baron Noirmont of France (*Histoire de la Chien—History of the Dog—*Vol II, p, 249) shares this same opinion:

> "In ancient Rome the fighting dogs and watch-dogs of the Tibetans (Serers) were well-known; they were enormously large and extremely ferocious. Seria (Tibet) is a very unique country. This country still produces,

even today, huge Tibet Mastiffs of colossal strength; their ferocity corresponds precisely to that described in the Latin verses

The Hunting Dogs of Ashurbanipal. The eager dogs strain at their leashes while one of the men carries nets. Ashurbanipal, a passionate hunter, was king of Assyria from 883-859 B.C. *British Museum*

of Gratius Faliscus: 'Sunt qui Seras alunt, genus intractabilis irae,'" ("Furthermore, the dogs which the Serers, or Tibetans, raise and breed are well-known: a wayward, head-strong, unruly breed, which is famous for its savage ferocity.")

Considerably older than written accounts of him, or of related breeds, are the pictorial repre-

A portion of a bas-relief from Ashurbanipal showing dogs hunting wild horses. *British Museum*

sentations that we possess from Assyria and Babylonia. Most of the probably 2,500-year-old dog pictures represent massive Mastiffs, one of which, discovered by Colonel H. Rawlinson in Birs Nimrud near Niniveh (Assyria) represents beyond all doubt a Tibet Mastiff.[10]

The exact origin of the large Mastiffs from India, or as the case may be, from the Himalayas or Tibet, which were found in Assyria prior to and during the Persian Empire (6th Century B.C.), seems to be dubious. On the other hand, the Greek historian Herodotus[11] (5th Century B.C.) reports that Cyrus had appropriated the income from several cities to be used for maintaining the breeding programs of his Dogs of India.[12]

Secondly, all the ancient documents agree on the point that a breed of especially massive, large dogs was derived from India. Thirdly, in all those regions which then comprised Assyria, Babylonia and ancient Persia, there is nowadays no sign of a flop-eared, short or long-coated Mastiff of the type which, in numerous pictures and representations on earthenware pottery or their fragments, have been preserved for us from antiquity.[13]

The homeland of the huge Mastiff-like dogs, which was closest to and could still be reached from Assyria, Babylonia and Persia, was the Himalayan Mountain region, or in the broadest sense: Tibet. It is strange that we have no pictures from the Greeks and Romans which could be clas-

This section of bas-relief from the palace of Ashurbanipal, at Nineveh, shows an ass hunt. *British Museum*

A terra-cotta dog cut into a slab in ancient Assyria. Note the cropped ears. The markings on the dog's side are his name, "Daan Rizsu."

sified as Tibet Mastiffs. Nevertheless, they knew about these dogs, as is documented in numerous passages found in ancient classical literature. However, as far as we know, Alexander the Great (356-323 B.C.) was the first, and not his legendary predecessors Bacchus or Hercules, who made the Greeks familiar with India, and thus with Tibet and its dogs.

It is generally assumed that Aristotle (384-322 B.C., Greek philosopher), who was the private tutor of Alexander the Great (King of Macedonia and conqueror of Greece, Egypt and the Persian Empire), was the first to mention, in any literature concerning the region of Tibet, a *dog* from that region.[14] Aristotle is the oldest noteworthy natural scientist whose works have remained preserved for us. Aristotle calls him the Dog of India, but obviously he was not personally familiar with this dog from first-hand observations, but from hearsay.

Aristotle had been told of this dog's wild ferocity; at the same time, he had heard about the "Chittah", the tamed hunting leopard, used for hunting in central Asia and in India. Aristotle must have confused the Dog of India with the "Chittah". The following statement about the Dog of India cannot be explained otherwise:

"It has also been told that the Dogs of India are produced by crossbreeding a tiger with

A terra-cotta plaque from Babylonia.

a dog bitch, but they are not first-generation offspring, but the offspring from the third cross-back breeding to the dog, since from the first generation after crossbreeding, the offspring are said to be too ill-tempered, wild and savage—indeed unruly. The dog bitches in season are led out into the desert, where they are bound with their leashes to large stones, and many are devoured until one of the wild animals, possessed by sufficient sexual urge, mates with the bitch."

Megasthenes was the war correspondent of Alexander the Great. (The military expedition to India and the conquest of King Porus at the Hydaspes took place in the year 327 B.C.) Megasthenes[15] was the first European who ever rendered precise descriptions concerning an Asi-

A plaster reproduction of a statue found near Athens.

atic dog, or as we call him, the Dog of India. In reality, these descriptions are, beyond all doubt, dealing with the Tibet Mastiff. Megasthenes mentions that this breed of dog had flop-ears, colossal bone structure, was muscular and massive with a huge, bulky head and broad muzzle.

A seal showing a crop eared Grecian war and hunting dog.

The descriptions used by Megasthenes have since then been quoted by many,[16] especially by English authors now in the 19th Century,[17] who linked these Dogs of India with the Tibetan Mastiff.

Although Curtius Rufus, who lived in the first century A.D. and who reported the deeds of Alexander the Great, did not describe the appearance of the Dog of India, he did write about the usefulness of this dog:

> "After crossing the Hydaspes and after conquering Porus, Alexander the Great came into the land of King Sopeithes. In this country there are superior hunting dogs, which, as they say, at first sight of game, stop barking immediately. These dogs are especially good for hunting lions. In order to make an eye-witness out of Alexander the Great with regard to the superb hunting qualities of these dogs, Sopeithes ordered his servants

to bring him an extraordinarily large lion and to let this lion be pursued by *four* dogs only. These dogs attacked the lion immediately, holding onto him

A pottery head of a dog found in Delos, around 200 B.C.

with their powerful jaw-grip. One of the king's hunting servants caught hold of a leg of one of these dogs, hanging with an iron grip on the lions' body. The servant attempted to pull the dog away from the lion, but instead, while doing so, he ripped the dog's entire leg off, since the dog would not let go of the lion. Since the dog did not react to this, the servant ripped off a second leg; and since he still would not loosen his iron grip on the lion, the servant severed one body part

Stone head of a Phoenician dog.

46

after the other from the dog's rump. In spite of this, the dog still kept his jaw-grip on the lion's body, although he was already dead now. This shows what an unbelievably passionate hunting instinct these dogs have for the lion hunt."

Strabo, the Greek geographer from Pontos, who died around the year 25 A.D., told the same story about the Tibetan dogs in the 15th Book, 1st Subdivision, Paragraph 31, of his geographical works. The entire country beyond the Hypanis was described best, but these descriptions were not reliable. He wrote that this country, through supernatural forces, had extraordinary animals and human-beings, such as the extremely long-lived Serers (Tibetans). He reported that even ebony was found there, as well as very courageous dogs, which would not turn loose of whatever they gripped between their teeth, using their extremely powerful jaws, until water was poured into their nostrils. Some of these dogs would roll their eyes in furious rage while biting, and sometimes these dogs' eyes would pop out of their sockets. He wrote that lions and bulls were always grabbed by these dogs immediately, and that once a bull had died when one of these dogs bit into his nose, even before the dog could be pulled away from him.

The Roman story-tellers and poets presenting hunting-tales also mention regularly in their depictions and portrayals the Dog of India, as he was at that time. It is a shame that these name-notations given him in the hunting-tales have little or no value for us, since they almost never include a description of the dog's appearance. More frequently, they only provide a mere glance at the dog's characteristics, as in the case of Gratius Faliscus, who offers no more regarding the dogs of the Tibetans than the verse quoted already on the first page of our book:

> "Sunt qui Seras alunt, genus intractabilis irae."

> ("Furthermore, the dogs which the Serers, or Tibetans, raise and breed are known; a wayward, headstrong, unruly breed, which is famous for its savage ferocity.")

We shall omit mentioning all the insignificant names given the Dog of India by Roman writers, for whom the Tibet Mastiff was well-known, since they are only worthless reiterations. However, we did bring from India the copy of a picture of dogs resembling Tibet Mastiffs: this picture is on a brick fragment from a building in India constructed during King Asoka's period (260-222 B.C.).

The original of this picture is found in western India's Sanchi Tope on one of the vaulted gates

A Molossus of the Romans, drawn from an ancient statue. It resembles the present day Albanian dogs, yet shows no resemblance to the Tibetan Mastiff or genuine German or Swiss type of Molossus.

leading into a Buddhist temple. There, richly adorned sculptures from the Buddhist period apparently represent the animals which, by that time, had been tamed or domesticated, or which were worshipped: for example, elephants, the water buffalo, camels, mountain sheep, broad-foreheaded dogs, imaginary lions or mythical animals.

These dogs shown in the sculptures are broad-foreheaded and flop-eared, with a long, mane-like coat on the front part of the body. In this picture, however, it is not difficult to recognize the Tibet Mastiff; disturbing in this picture is only the unnatural pig-like curly tail with bristles at the tail-tip. Strangely enough, the imaginary lions of these sculptures have quite similar tails of this ridiculous type. Pictures of dogs on buildings in India, to which we have access, are extremely rare, not only on all ancient buildings, but also on those built more recently. Most of the few rare pictures of dogs are so bizarre that they are insignificant for tracing back a history of the Tibet Mastiff.

Evidence for the slight significance of the dog in the plains of India is found. For example, the bronze statues copied nowadays in Benares, showing the guardian god of protection for the city of Bairo Nath, riding on a dog's back. The tutelary god here is riding on an indescribable flop-eared, long-coated animal, which is supposed to represent a dog; more cannot be said, and this also applies to the dogs on the small, old pastel pictures and the ivory paintings of ancient times in India. Only in a collection of old miniature pictures dating back to the end of the 18th Century, are dogs pictured, whose breed we can identify by erudition. K. E. von

The Hindu god Bhairava, commonly portrayed in the company of a black dog.

Yamantaka stands on his dog. This brass object hails from the 1800s, in Nepal, and is remarkably similar to the object from Benares, India to which Siber refers.

Ujfalvy received this collection from Radja Sham Sing of Chamba in Kashmir: it portrays a story about his great-grandfather. One of the dogs pictured is probably a Tazi, a long-coated sight-hound of Central Asia, similar to a Borzoi; we can classify the other dog as one closely related to and resembling the Tibet Mastiff for the following reasons: this dog has the fifth toe ("wolf-claw") on his hind paws; he is long-coated; he has drooping ears; he carries his tail, like the Tibet Mastiff, over his back; he seems to be very large and strong. Ujfalvy described this dog in the following manner:

> "A dumpy, almost dwarf-like person is leading a large, bulky, white-colored dog on a line; this dog is almost as large as the person leading him."

This small picture, of course, does not provide us with much information; at most, we can judge that this dog was either very popular or that he was considered valuable enough to receive the honor of being immortalized in a picture. From the literature from India, Dr. B Langkavel of Hamburg mentions the following with reference to the Tibet Mastiff:

A drawing copied from the miniature picture in Chamba of Kashmir, India, by Ujfalvy.

"The dogs of Tibet were probably the ones which in Ramaj II 70 21 the grandfather Acvapati presented in honor to the brother of Rame Bharata: these were the large-bodied dogs raised and bred in the palace, which were gifted with the power and strength of the tiger."

Taken from *Der Hund,*(Vol. IX, page 82)

As a matter of fact, the oldest writings about the dogs of Tibet are not found in European, but in Chinese literature:

"In the year 1121 before the beginning of our chronology, a people named *Liu* living in the west of China sent a dog of Tibetan breeding called the "Ngao" to Wou-Wang, the Emperor of China. According to Chinese historians of Chou-King, this dog was four feet tall and trained to track down human beings, as was often the case at that time in western India."[18]

Dr. Langkavel reports in an article about Tibetan dogs that at the time of Marco Polo, in the 13th Century, Tibetan rulers sent dogs called "Liu-Ngao" to China. These dogs were the size of donkeys and capable of overpowering tigers. The Chinese annals of the Han Dynasty (142-87 B.C.) are,

Marco Polo returning home from his travels accompanied by his faithful Tibetan Mastiff. From *The Tibetan Mastiff, Legendary Guardian of the Himalayas*, OTR Publications.

according to the same authority,[19] said to depict the Tibetan dogs as being as large as donkeys; but in this source, they are mentioned as being red in

An extraordinary painting of a Tibetan Mastiff from the 1600s, by an unknown Chinese artist.

color, which proves that already at that time *red* Tibet Mastiffs existed, in addition to the frequently found blacks with red markings.

A porcelain Chinese guard dog from the 1700s. *From Ash*

Naturally, Marco Polo, the famous European traveler of the Middle Ages, from Venice, Italy, who dictated the classical tales regarding his travels in the year 1298 and revised these stories in the year 1307, noticed and observed the Tibet Mastiff. His observations concerning Tibetan customs, the peculiar custom that the women before marriage were to be as sexually unchaste and promiscuous as possible, the existence of the musk-deer, and many more interesting observations, are still today so true and correct in Tibet that one can only fully believe and trust his observations concerning the dogs he watched there at that time.

A terra-cotta Mastiff tomb dog from the Tang Dynasty. Such statues protected the buried from evil spirits.

In the old French text of the year 1865 by M. G, Pauthier, Chapter 114, the following is written, which was translated into English in *The Book of Marco Polo*, London, in the year 1872:

"I must also relate that in this country (Tibet), many animals exist that produce musk. The people of this country own a large number of strong, powerful, noble dogs, which are valuable servants in catching and hunting the musk-deer.

The people of Tibet are very poor; they raise Mastiffs, as large as donkeys, which are excellent for hunting wild animals, namely the wild Yaks, which are big and mean animals. They also raise other breeds of hunting dogs, and they own excellent tamed hunting falcons."

Chapter Three

Recent History

From the days of Marco Polo onwards, the Tibet Mastiff was not mentioned, strangely enough, for 500 years, until the very end of the 18th Century; the first who reacquainted us with these dogs was Samuel Turner, who, by order of the East India Company, traveled through Bhutan,[20] which lies in the eastern Himalayas of northern India, into Tibet. This was around the year 1800. From this point on, we shall give our readers, in spite of the many redundant or repetitive reports during the 18th Century, all the information which the envoys who traveled there from the East India Company recalled and documented. Although all these reports contain almost without exception the same information, we believe that they should be reprinted, because they deal with specific, important characteristics of the Tibet Mastiff, and they give us a complete picture of this breed, with which very few of our readers are directly acquainted. Samuel Turner wrote the following:

"At the border of Bhutan and Tibet, high in the Himalayas, I encountered a group of Tartar shepherds, who always lived in tents and did nothing other than let their livestock graze. Their herds consisted of 200 to 300 heavy-tailed Yaks. During the day, these yaks grazed in the surrounding mountains. At night they were called and driven together, tied to ropes and fastened with pegs in double rows in front of their tents. Here they were guarded by two large Tibet Mastiffs.

"In one of the poor Tibetan villages, I, out of curiosity, roved about between the houses; and since everything was quite calm and completely silent, I entered an enclosure constructed from stones, which, to my astonishment, served as a livestock-shed. To my surprise, just as I walked in, a huge dog jumped up and ran towards me. This dog possessed, if his courage were equal to his size, the strength and power to fight with a lion. He held me back, with his roaring growl, frenzied barking and ferocity, to the stone boundary of the enclosure. At first I was very startled and terrified; but since I then remembered that dogs usually do not attack until they notice that someone is afraid of them, I stood absolutely still. Had I fled, he

A Tibetan Mastiff photographed in his homeland. From The German Shepherd Dog in Word and Picture, by Von Stephanitz.

would probably have leaped after me, ripping me to pieces, before anybody could have rescued me. In the meantime, somebody came out of the house, and the dog was very quickly calmed down and brought to silence.

"In Bhutan, in front of the country villa belonging to the Radja of Tassisudon, there stood to the left a row of wooden cages, in which a number of large dogs were kept. These dogs were very fierce, strong and violent. They barked in a very raging, terrifying manner. They were from Tibet; and they were either vicious by nature or incensed with pent-up energy from being confined to these cages. They behaved in such a turbulent, ferocious manner that it would have been extremely dangerous to even approach their brittle cages, if their caretakers had not been present nearby."

The German author Dr. F. L. Walter, who wrote his booklet entitled *Der Hund (The Dog)* in the year 1817, groups the following breeds together as Mastiffs: the Bull-Biter or Molossus, the St. Bernard, the English Mastiff, the Great Dane and the Tibet Mastiff, which he gives the Latin name *Canis familiaris tibetius*. However, he only makes the following statement: "The Tibet Mastiff has not yet been described."

Bryan Hodgson, the famous English zoologist of the early 1800s, studied the mammals of the Himalayan foot-hills, at the end of the 1820s. Later in his famous book *Drawings of Nepalese Animals*, he repeatedly made reference to the Tibet Mastiff, or, as he usually called this breed, "the Bhotea Dogs". In a report dealing with the animals of Nepal, which was published in the periodical entitled *Journal-Asiat. Soc. Bengal*, Volume I, page 342,[21] in the year 1832, he described the Tibet Mastiff in the following manner:

"A noble, aristocratic breed, usually called the Nepal Dog, is found only in Kachar, which is the only suitable location in Nepal in which this breed can live and thrive. He was imported from Tibet, the region in which he is at home and where there are, in various areas, several varieties of this breed. The variety from Lhassa is the most beautiful variety, and is almost always black with tan legs and a fifth or "false toe" front and rear.[22]

"The "Mustang" variety is much smaller, bright red in color, with small eyes; this variety does not have the rear fifth toes. Even in Kachar these dogs age and deteriorate very rapidly; the heat of Nepal's interior regions is just as unbearable for these dogs as for a human-being from Tibet. This ap-

"Tibetan Mastiffs, 5-clawed and 4-clawed var." by Bryan Hodgson. Hodgson, a respected naturalist, first became acquainted with the breed while living in Nepal, in 1842.

pears to be the dog whose extraordinary strength amazed and astonished Alexander the Great and his Greeks many centuries ago. This breed is found throughout the entire country of Tibet. This breed is correctly classified within Cuvier's 3rd Class of the Dog Family "Caninae", but must be reclassified under the *Mastiffs* instead of under the Bulldogs.

"His large body framework, a massive, short muzzle, long coat, deeply-set eyes, ears completely folded down and the 5th claw, a dewclaw (at least characteristic of the Lhassa variety), seem decisive for this classification. The main characteristic of his skull consists in the great extension of the longitudinal and transversal cristae."

The *Illustrated London News* published the illustration of ancient Assyrian dogs of the type used for hunting. The text accompanying this illustration is as follows:

"These dogs are of large body framework, of a very wild, fierce appearance, with small drooping ears, a thick head and strong, powerful legs; they greatly resemble the most massive and ferocious of our old Mastiffs."

In addition. in the periodical *Asiatic Researches*, Vol, XVII, page 14, published in the year 1832, Hodgson is said to have presented a detailed report concerning two dog breeds found in Bhotea (Bhutan). Unfortunately, we were not able to obtain a copy of this source material.

The next writer to mention the Tibet Mastiff, and who is said to have pictured him, is Mr. Bennett, who described the breed according to the specimens exhibited at the Menagerie of the London Tower in the 1830s. This zoo-like institute kept a couple of Tibet Mastiffs for their regular animal shows, probably the first Tibet Mastiffs that had ever been brought to Europe. They created a great sensation there. Unfortunately, in our copy of the show program for Bennett's Tower Menagerie, the vignette and description of the Tibet Mastiff is missing. We must therefore turn to Colonel Hamilton Smith, who wrote about the Tibet Mastiff in the year 1840, and to the writer Youatt. Both used the Bennett publications as their source material, and each of them depicted our Tibet Mastiff.

Colonel Hamilton Smith writes the following:

"The Mastiff of Tibet is larger than the English Mastiff, has a thick, bulky head, a prominent occipital bone at the rear of the skull, deeply drooping ears, wrinkles above the eye-brows and on the cheeks; the ears

The "Mastiff of Thibet" from the 1840 book *The History of Quadrapeds.*

are well-rounded and hang down completely; the neck is strong; the back is slightly arched. The tail is bent over backwards, turning toward the dog's back: it is covered with long hair, and just as the long, coarse body-coat, the tail is deep black with some lighter shadings on the extremities. Above the eyes and on the cheeks and legs, reddish-brown spots and markings are evident." [The picture of a wonderful wood-carving and an excellent description of these noble dogs are found in Mr. Bennett's publication entitled *Gardens and Menageries of the Zoological Society.*]

In Mr. Bennett's article, several less significant varieties of the Tibet Mastiff are mentioned, which are bred in different locations and regions of the Himalayan Mountains. According to Brian Hodgson, Tibet Mastiffs do not thrive down in the Katmandu Valley, however.

In the excellent publication entitled *The Dog* by Youatt, of which the German translation by von Weiss is available, the Tibet Mastiff was described at the very beginning in the following words:

> "Mr. Bennett furnished us, in his instructive, entertaining description of the animal garden at the London Tower Menagerie, with the best information about the noble Tibet Mastiff. Our illustration offers a life-like picture of this breed.

> "These dogs are bred on the high plateaus of the Himalayan Mountains in Tibet. The Bhoteas, or inhabitants of Bhutan, who raise them there with great care and dedication, come down into the plains at certain times of the year, in order to sell borax and musk. Their wives stay at home with their livestock herds, which graze there, guarded by their Tibet Mastiffs. These dogs guard and protect all the larger settlements in Tibet.

> "Every person who has ever described this

breed says that they are large, beautiful, fierce animals, and that they cannot stand strangers. Outside of their native homeland, they are said to degenerate, deteriorate and age rapidly. The specimens which are now kept in the London Tower Menagerie's animal garden, which is actually like a small zoo, have not shown any signs of ferocity at all. One of these dogs looked very noble and proud, and this very individual had an extremely amiable, outgoing disposition.

"These dogs are deep black in color, with sightly gray shading on their sides. Only the paws and a spot above each eye are of a deep rust color or light brown. The muzzle is broad and short, similar to that of the Molossus (Bull-Biter). Their lips sag somewhat more than the lips of the Molossus. Over the entire rump, an unusual coat flaccidity can be felt."

The next writer after Youatt, who published information about the Tibet Mastiff in his book entitled *The Dog*, in the year 1845, was the Englishman Martin:

"The Tibet Mastiff surpasses the English Mastiff with regard to size; furthermore, he has a much more dismal, grim facial expression than the English Mastiff, which results from the fact that the skin above the dog's eyes forms deep wrinkles,

"The Thibet Dog" from *The Dog,* by Youatt.

which extend down over both cheeks, and from the dog's deeply sagging lips. These mighty dogs are the guards of the people living high up in the Himalayan plateaus and valleys in and near Tibet. The dog's body is covered with long, rough or coarse hair, which is mainly black in color; yellowish shadings are found on the dog's extremities, i.e. his legs, his pelvic region and above his eye-brows. His tail is heavily coated and bends back over his back. These dogs are extremely devoted and attached to their masters, the inhabitants of Bhutan or Bhotea; on the other hand, however, they are quite vicious to strangers, namely also to Europeans, whom they will violently attack."

According to Youatt and other writers, various less significant varieties of the Tibet Mastiff are distributed over the entire chain of the Himalayas. These dogs deteriorate and age rapidly, if they are taken from the bleak, rugged mountainous terrain down into a milder climate zone. This degeneration, however, does not only result from the climate change, but also, just as much, from the change in nutrition, because in the plains and foothills of India the Hindus live, who, according to their religion, are not permitted to kill an animal; therefore, these Hindus very rarely eat meat (only, for example, animals sacrificed and animals that died spontaneously, such as fish taken from the water). Other than Hindus

An early etching of a Tibetan Mastiff. Source unknown.

only Mohammedans, who hate dogs, are found in the plains and foothills of India. Consequently, none of these people are capable of sufficiently nourishing these big dogs that are accustomed to better, more nutritional food. No other domesticated animal will be stunted in growth as quickly as a dog, if not provided with sufficient nutrition.

A pack of such dogs recently brought to London by Dr. Wallich, where they were presented to the London Zoo, died soon after their arrival there. On the other hand, a few years ago, we saw a wonderful pair of these dogs at the Botanical Garden in Paris. Marco Polo mentioned the Tibet Mastiff. The Bhoteas, or folk of Bhutan, who possess the oldest varieties of this breed, are a very rugged, weather-tanned people, thick-set and dumpy in build, but very strong, resolute and persevering. Their clothing is adapted to the bleak, cold climate, in which they live: it consists of furs, hides and woolen material. The men cultivate the land and raise sheep. At certain times of the year, they come down into the valleys, in order to sell or trade their agricultural products. Sometimes they even travel as far as Calcutta. During this time, the women remain at home, protected by the dogs, which guard their settlements.

In the 1850s, the famous English botanist Hooker traveled through Sikkim, Bhutan and even reached the outskirts of Tibet. He became very thoroughly acquainted with the Tibet Mastiff on this occasion. In his splendid work entitled *Himalayan Journals*, published in London in the year 1854, (Part I, p. 203 and following), he even pictures a Tibet Mastiff. The head in that picture is said to closely resemble the head of an English Mastiff (Bull-Biter). He describes the Tibet Mastiff as follows:

"The caravans of the Tibetans are marching in good order; we are now among goats and sheep, each of which is carrying his two little bags of salt; beside them is walking—deliberately, circumspectly, calmly—the huge, powerful, bull-necked Tibet Mastiff, who is loaded down like all the other animals. His long-coated, heavy tail, which is turned back in a pronounced arch over his back, his broad collar made of red wool, bound around his neck and hanging down over his shoulders, contrasts well with his lustrous coat. Unquestionably, he is the most noble member of the entire caravan, particularly when his coat is of fine, silky texture, since there are some specimens of the breed that have harsh, rougher coats and are merely of a dark color, with a rather plain, unimpressive appearance. Loaded down and marching in the caravan, the Tibet Mastiff does not seem to be in his true position, since he is neither guarding nor fulfilling watch-dog responsibilities: he knows that during the day-time neither the goats and sheep nor the Yaks need his guardianship and care, because they are completely peaceable; therefore, he participates patiently in the teamwork and carries loads like they do. The Tibet Mastiff serves as their guardian only during the night."

In another article concerning the great high-plateau of Tibet, published in the year 1848, Hooker mentions briefly a Tibet Mastiff, or as he called this breed, the Bhotea Dog. He was located at that time at a pass near the Lattschen River at the border to Tibet, in the tent of the Subah or village chief. His dog named "Kintschin", bound to his leash outside the tent, started barking furiously at an enormous Bhotea Dog. This Bhotea Dog was a very noble specimen, who would gladly have ripped Hooker's watch-dog "Kintschin" to shreds.

A most significant German natural scientist and expert on dog breeds was Professor Dr. Leopold Fitzinger of Vienna, Austria. Before his death a few years ago [1891], he described the Tibet Mastiff, which he called the *Canis molossus tibetanus*, in the following manner:

"This breed is also a pure, non-mongrelized variety of the Molossus (Bull-Biter), whose unique characteristics are the result of selective adaptations to his geographical environment, and to climatic influences thereof. This dog evolved within the middle regions of Asia, where he later adapted particularly to his present native homeland, Tibet.

"This elegant breed, distinguished by its strength and power, presents in its overall body anatomy an unmistakable similarity to the large European Bull-Biter *(Canis molossus major)*. It differs, on the other hand, from this European type not only in having a stronger body construction and in being considerably larger, but also in other important characteristics. Even the largest specimens of the common European Mastiff varieties *(Canis molossus mastivus)* do not attain the size of the Tibet Mastiff.

"The head is larger, the back of the head (occiput) is more pronounced, and the strongly arched forehead or upper skull presents above the eye-brows a deep furrow or wrinkle. The muzzle is broader and more blunt, yet somewhat less distended; the lips are longer and therefore more deeply sagging. The skin of the cheek region is looser, the ears are longer and more rounded, and the eyes are somewhat smaller. The neck is shorter and even thicker; the abdomen is more rounded; and the tail, which is usually carried over the back, bent toward the dog's back and front of the body, appears to be, as a result of the profuse coating, considerably thicker and almost bushy. The fur on the sides is flaccid, and the body coating in general is much longer; on the tail, the coat is the longest, especially on the tail's underside, where long fringes are formed.

An interesting early Tibetan Mastiff etching. Source unknown.

"The color of the body coating is deep black, and on the sides somewhat grayish, and only the paws and a small, round spot above each eye are bright rust-yellow or light brown in color.

"The English call this dog "the Mastiff of Tibet", and the French named him the "Dogue du Tibet". Although these strikingly large, strong dogs were already known in Europe during the ages of the ancient Greeks and Romans, when they were described by Aristotle, Strabo and Plinius, when they were called *Canis indicus (Dog of India)*, later renamed *Canis hyrcanus* by Gratius Faliscus, they remained completely unknown to us up until around the 1820s.

"Aristotle considered the Tibet Mastiff to be a bastard produced by crossbreeding a domesticated dog with a tiger or with some other wild animal similar to a dog. He believed that these dogs were not produced from the first generation after crossbreeding, but from the third generation after breeding the bastard back to the domesticated dog, in order to produce tame ones, since the first-generation product from the crossbreeding was still completely wild."

Chapter Four

The Tibetan Mastiff Today

For excellent information regarding the Tibet Mastiff derived from first-hand observations, we are indebted to the Austrian officer Kreitner, who, as an official historiographer, accompanied Count Bela Szechenyi on his long journey to Eastern Asia and who wrote a splendid travel book, from which we have quoted the following documentary information:

"Already in China we had heard so much about the beautiful Tibetan dogs, that I was really looking forward to becoming acquainted with these animals. And, indeed, they do definitely deserve this praise. The Tibet Mastiffs resemble the most beautiful Newfoundlands in many ways. The head of the Tibetan dogs is considerably larger, however, and gains impressive, menacing fierceness through the mane-like, upstanding neck-coating. This impression is intensified when the native owner puts on the dog's red, wreath-like collar made from Yak hair. The color of the Tibet Mastiff ranges from black to a light golden brown or red, but the vast majority of them are black in color with rust-colored markings. They are in general quite vicious; and if kept chained inside the house, they frequently cause the air to vibrate with their deep-throated barks. During an attack, they wag their tails incessantly, in a frenzied manner. As sheep-dogs or with Yak caravans, they maintain peace and order, providing simultaneously for the necessary security through their watchful vigilance. Count Szechenyi purchased three splendid Tibet Mastiffs: two males named 'Dschandu' and 'Dsamu', as well as a female named 'Dsama'. 'Dschandu' and 'Dsama' were not only trainable, but also endured the long journey to Europe over land and sea without endangering their health and longevity. At the present time, they are counted as the most reliable guards at the castle of Count Szechenyi on the beautiful lake Neusiedler See in Zinkendorf, Austria.

"Dschandu," a male Tibetan Mastiff, imported by Count Belá Széchenyi. Photo by Rosa Jenik, Vienna, Austria. A drawing of this dog may be seen on page 117.

This grainy photo is of "Dsama," the female brought to Austria by Count Belá Széchenyi. See also the drawing of "Dsama" on page 117.

"The other male 'Dsamu' had a quite different behavior pattern. As a definite enemy of all Europeans, he would not tolerate having a single one of us near him; he even bit the count repeatedly, who tried to tame him by hand-feeding him. On such an occasion, he lacerated the count's right hand severely.

"At almost every location that we had our night quarters, 'Dsamu' provided us with food supplies by mercilessly biting through the vertebral column of every chicken and pig that strayed into his proximity. However, when 'Dsamu' so severely mutilated a poor old woman in Bamo, who had threatened to hit him with a stick, his fate was sealed: Count Szechenyi shot him on the spot."[23]

Dr. Langkavel of Hamburg, Germany, to whom we are indebted for so much interesting information about dog breeds found outside of Europe, described in the year 1892 in the *Neue Deutsche Jagdzeitung (New German Hunter's Magazine)* the Tibet Mastiff in great detail, The following is an excerpt from this article:

"The Tibet Mastiff. In the Himalayas, that immense, vast chain of uniform mountains, of which dozens of peaks attain altitudes higher than seven kilometers or 4.4 miles and whose average altitude does not considerably exceed that of the adjoining Tibetan plateau, we find this unique dog breed. Tibet, over double the size of Germany and Austria-Hungary combined, has only been partially explored by Europeans up until now. It would be amazing if, in a country of such vast dimensions, the watch-dogs of the nomads, the Tibet Mastiff, were uniform as a breed in all of its different regions. Just as there is at present scarcely a group of people on earth that is ethnically pure, the domesticated animals, through contact with the

animals of other groups of people, have not remained unmixed, either; and from the various descriptions of these animals, which travelers have provided, we notice that at least in the border areas different strains, if not varieties, of the Tibet Mastiff appear."

How considerably our knowledge regarding the Tibet Mastiff has increased during the last decades can be seen from a comparison of this article with one describing the Tibet Mastiff that was published ten years ago, in 1887, in the magazine of the Verein für Hundezucht und Dressur im Konigreich Bohmen (the Club for Dog Breeding and Training in the Kingdom of Bohemia). Most tourists who have traveled to Tibet have reported the height of the Tibet Mastiff as being comparable to that of our donkeys. The Tibet Mastiffs found in Ladak, Tibet, are said to attain a height that is double the height of the larger Hindustani dogs of northern India.

The dogs of the Tibetan gold miners, as described by Carl Ritter, are also of this size. The descriptions given by the men with whom Max Siber conversed[24] also allow us to draw the conclusion that the Tibet Mastiffs in Tibet's interior regions are of a colossal size, since these men did not consider Max Siber's huge St. Bernard bitch to be anything extraordinary at all. They told him that they had dogs of this size at home, in large numbers.

Jule described the Tibet Mastiff as being as large as the Newfoundland, and Gill reported that the 3-year-old Tibet Mastiff he had seen was four feet in length, from the tip of the nose to the onset of the tail, and had a height at the withers measuring two feet and ten inches. H. von Schlagintweit said that he also saw a medium-sized variety during his trip to Tibet, but this was probably nothing other than one of the hunting dogs, which are also found rather frequently in Tibet.

The coat is, according to all sources, long and rather rough. Only Gill saw dogs with shorter hair and coats of medium length. During the winter, all of these Tibetan watch-dogs have a soft, dense undercoat, which insulates them like a blanket. If they are taken down into the plains of India, they soon shed their long coats, begin to appear sickly and seldom survive even a second hot summer there.

The skin color of many Tibet Mastiffs is said to be black, likewise the coat color. But there is considerable variation with regard to coat color: black with rust-red spots above the eyes, also occasionally appearing on the chest and legs; then there are some that are black with rust-brown markings of extensive measure; some are light brown or golden red; others are brown with yellow markings. In addition, some are fawn-colored or deep red: these are even mentioned in ancient Chinese writings which are over 2,000 years old.

The Lhasa variety is black with yellow-brown markings. Some of these blacks have extended, elongated yellowish-brown spots which appear as stripes above the eyes, on the legs and on the lips. Others are dark-colored with a black saddle. Hodgson is the only writer who observed one single dog having a pale, wolf-like gray color. The enormously large, bulky head is much larger than that of the Newfoundland. One could almost say that the Tibet Mastiff's head is disproportionate.

The lips of the Tibet Mastiff sag. The eyes are deeply set, with bloodshot conjunctivae. The ears are connected flatly to their point of attachment at the skull. The neck-coating is upstanding and mane-like. The legs are smooth-coated. Dewclaws are not seen exclusively in the Lhasa variety, but all Tibet Mastiffs have them, as well as the other mountain dogs of India and some of the Chinese breeds. (They are missing, which is a well-known fact, in the pure Pariah dogs of India, in the Battak Spitz of Sumatra and in other breeds of southeast Asia, according to M. Siber and G. Schweinfurth.)

The bushy tail is always carried upwards over the dog's back, and as a result of this carriage, the coat on the back is abraded here and there, so that it may appear short in certain places.

With regard to the breed group, the big black Mongolian dogs, the mountain dogs of Kashmir that are the size of Hungarian Shepherds, which have long, bushy tails and fine, dense undercoats below their long guard hair, and the watch-dogs of eastern Nan Shan may all be grouped together with the Tibet Mastiff as distantly related breeds, even if they do differ from the Tibet Mastiff with regard to their adaptations to climate as well as to geographical and ecological influences. Tibet Mastiffs have been sent to China, as far as we know, since the twelfth century, as presents on very special occasions. But most of the Tibet Mastiffs sent to China have been kept strictly confined to small cages, where they agonize until they die, mourning and longing for the free unrestrained life to which they had been accustomed.

Gill reported having witnessed this in his publication. Also in Upper Burma, dogs of this group are found, as well as in Kumaon; and the Dog of Nepal is also probably closely related to this group of dogs. If a dog from Tibet is sold to an Englishman, the price is usually around 200 marks *(this would be $2,000 in 1995 dollars-ed. note);* the Tibetans are happy with 60 marks *($600 in 1995 dollars-ed. note),* from a Chinese. The high price, however, is surely not the reason that this breed is seen so rarely in Europe. Alexander Hosie tells us in his book entitled *Three Years in Western China,* which was published in the year 1889, that after he had become acquainted with the strong, powerful dogs there, he had intended to purchase one. He had decided to refrain from this, however, since only a Tibetan is capable of curb-

A magnificent drawing of a Tibetan Mastiff by famed dog artist Arthur Wardle.

ing the ferocity of this breed. Up until the point of transferal into an English ship, the purchased dog would have required a native Tibetan to subdue and take care of this dog. The criteria which we use for tending to domesticated animals is out of place in Tibet. The Yaks are, in this regard, not at all comparable to our cattle; and this also applies to our patient moorland sheep in contrast with the Tibetan Purik sheep, which climb as pack animals in long caravans through the most difficult mountain passes, arriving in the Kulu Valley with borax. The attendants and guides of these half-wild animals are the Tibet Mastiffs, which are necessary for protecting these herds against the attacks of wild animals at night. Unceasingly, two or three of them circle round a herd, barking deeply while doing so. These dogs are so savage and head-strong that they will attack and rip any stranger to shreds, be this a human-being or a beast of prey, that approaches the camp site after dark. These dogs all wear a sturdy iron-spiked collar in order to be a match for a leopard in a fight. When travelers approach a village during the day-time, the women come out of the lodgings there, hold their dogs tight and remain seated, as depicted by Henderson, on the dog's head until the traveler has departed from the settlement; otherwise, the Tibet Mastiffs there would rip the rider and his horse to pieces. In the dark, reports Markham, even the inhabitants of the village would not dare to leave their dwellings, because at night these savage watch-dogs do not first scent out whether or not it is their master whom they see, but attack anybody who appears.

Well-known are the tales of antiquity, according to which such strong, courageous fighting dogs found in the Caucasus Mountains, in Persia and in Afghanistan, even defeated lions. Marco Polo reported having witnessed such mighty, ferocious dogs in the Asiatic highlands, but he meant "tigers" and "leopards" instead of "lions", when he used the word "leones" with reference to the animals with which these dogs fought. The reasons why the European continent only very rarely received Tibet Mastiffs can be traced back, first, to their ferocity; secondly, to the trouble of transporting them to Europe; and thirdly, to the difficulty in keeping an animal healthy that had always been used to living in the mountains of Tibet, after being brought into our European regions only slightly above sea-level.

Henderson and Hume report that some Tibet Mastiffs had been brought to England with great difficulty around the year 1870 and had been used as watch-dogs there. How long they were able to live there, I do not know. Twelve years ago, Count Szechenyi brought two Tibet Mastiffs to his homeland Austria-Hungary from his trip to Asia. He used them to guard his castle in Zinkendorf at Neusiedler See in Austria.

A Tibetan Mastiff tied to a dwelling in Tibet. *From Hutchinson's Dog Encyclopedia.*

The largest dog in England at the moment (1892), "the giant dog", is a Tibet Mastiff owned by a Mr. Wilson. Also, in the Far East there are well-to-do animal enthusiasts who either develop small zoological gardens for themselves ŏr who build up magnificent, large kennels of dogs, where they produce beautiful specimens in numerous different breeds. The Prince of Batang belonged to the first type during the mid-1870s. He much preferred to occupy himself with the breeding of horses, mules, cats and dogs than with the administration of his land. Among his beautiful dogs, a Tibet Mastiff was especially outstanding on account of his extremely large size. He even owned a marmot and a bear. His son was also an animal lover "with profound understanding", for when Gustav Kreitner showed him a microscope for the first time and demonstrated how to use it, he immediately felt up under his shirt, fished out a louse, put it under the cover glass, and after long microscopy, he exclaimed that it looked "like a clumsy dragon caught in a deep pit".

When Mr. Robert Moss King was living in Jammu with his wife, who published a very interesting book in 1891 entitled *The Wife of a Government Official in India*, he heard that the Maharajah of Jammu had a kennel of 200 to 300 dogs, among which all breeds were represented. Unfortunately, the kennel was too far away from his home and there was not enough time to make a frequent kennel visit there, but the English did get to see a few of these splendid dogs trained for the bear hunt. These dogs were probably Tibet Mastiff mixes or blends, having resulted from crossbreeding with the Tibet Mastiff.

Each of the six dogs, attached to a special chain leash, was separately led out each day on a long stroll by one of the Maharajah's servants.

How closely the Tibet Mastiff is linked with the life of the Tibetans will be evident to us from the following episode:

> General von Prschewalski encountered several shamanistic soothsayers (prophets and medicine men) in northern Tibet who slayed their obediently chained dog with great ceremony and exorcism, cut up the dog's body and then started prophesying. In Sikkim, the household gods or deities are pictured with grotesque, distorted faces, riding on giant dogs.

Schlagintweit, the German reporter who had traveled to the Himalayas during the 1870s, writes the following with regard to Tibet:

> "Among the domesticated animals frequently found in Tibet are the cat and the dog. The dog breed there is medium-sized and dark in color. Most frequently, the back is black. The front part of the head and stom-

ach are somewhat lighter brown in color. These dogs are mainly kept by shepherds, not only out on the meadows, but also where they are even more necessary: on the mountainous roads and paths, where they lead and guard the herds of sheep carrying loads of goods down into the valleys. They climb over the mountain passes just as the sheep do, usually never showing any signs of being affected by the decrease in air pressure. South of the Himalayas, dogs are rarely kept as pets or for utility purposes. The natives there are not familiar with hunting dogs."

A village woman ties her Tibetan Mastiff to her house. Note the furry collar made of yak hair. From A Cultural History of Tibet, by David Snellgrove and Hugh Richardson. Courtesy of Weidenfeld & Nicholson, Ltd., London.

In another passage, Schlagintweit makes the following interesting comment:

"Among the birds hunted there, the Tibetan partridge was the most numerous type. At Korzog I took along one of the shepherds' dogs with me, since his master also accompanied me. Although the dog was not of a hunting breed and was so restless that I had to hold his leash with a tight grip, he was still quite useful to me, since he caught scent of a covey of partridges at a distance of over 200 feet away. Here, at more than 15,400 feet altitude, the thin air was conducive to and favorable for vaporizing the animals' scents; even gaseous suspensions, such as fog-banks, were rapidly vaporized and diminished. Wounded birds had a temperature of 41-42 degrees Centigrade (105.8-107.6 degrees Fahrenheit). But as soon as the birds were dead, they lost their body temperature much more rapidly than they do here in Central Europe, since the Himalayan atmosphere is much thinner and cooler. But the vaporization of scent also ceased very soon up there and if a partridge was not found immediately after being killed, the same dog could not locate this bird even 20 feet away."

The English and French publishers of dog books, even the standard works incorporating canine breed research, present all the above information in various repetitions. The most detailed publication is by Corsincon, the pen-name of Hugh Dalziel, in his article entitled "The Tibet Mastiff":

"This breed is seen rather rarely in England, thus only once has a Tibet Mastiff been represented at an English dog show. This breed is, however, so mighty and beautiful that propagation and expansion of the Tibet Mastiff here in England should be welcomed. The Tibet Mastiff is well worth fostering and cultivating; even the breed's noble appearance in itself would be justification enough for this. Through their skill and intelligence, English breeders would be capable of further enhancing, developing and intensifying the good characteristics of these dogs, for example even more superior body anatomy and even more noble external appearance.

"In their native homeland, these Tibet Mastiffs serve primarily as guardians of the livestock herds and their masters' settlements. A half dozen of these dogs ready to fight, their bushy tails erect and the coat on their backs bristled up, are capable of providing excellent defense against robbers and enemies, be they human beings or beasts of prey.

"Generally speaking, the Tibet Mastiff resembles the English Mastiff with regard to external appearance, although his long, dense coat and his black color stand in sharp contrast to the reddish or fawn-colored English Mastiffs with their fine, short, smooth coats.

"Drawings of "Siring" depict a magnificent Tibet Mastiff specimen. He is a representative from a superior brace of two such dogs, owned by the Prince of Wales, who exhibited the dogs at Alexandra Palace in the year 1875. The two dogs in this brace were well-matched, and they were admired very much by all the spectators there, although Siring was obviously the better of the two dogs.

"With regard to size, the Tibet Mastiff is somewhat smaller than the English Mastiff, although his long coat causes him to appear larger than he really is.

"Both dogs owned by the Prince of Wales were well-built, possessing well-set tails of excellent form and carriage. These two dogs had excellent backs, wide loins, deep chests, powerful hindquarters; in addition, they stood on strong, straight legs of heavy bone structure.

"The coats of the Tibet Mastiffs, approximately as long as those of the Newfoundland, are very dense—not fine and silky, but simply long without being coarse in texture. The color is black with rust-red markings; the large, strong tail is nicely arched over the dog's back.

"The head, which renders the Tibet Mastiff his special appearance, is quite different from that of the English Mastiff, but has only slight resemblance to the head of a Bloodhound. It would be more correct to regard the Tibet Mastiff's head as an intermediate between the heads of the English Mastiff and the Bloodhound. The Tibet Mastiff's skull is shorter than that of the Bloodhound, but yet not as massive as the skull of the English Mastiff. His ears are small, like the ears of

The famous Siring, imported by the Prince of Wales, in 1876. From *British Dogs*, by Drury.

the English Mastiff, but his eyes are deep-set like the eyes of the Bloodhound (or even more like the eyes of the St. Bernard. The red conjunctivae of the eyes are visible, the well-developed lips are saggingly overhanging, just as precipitously as the lips of the Bloodhound. In addition, the Tibet Mastiff has a pronounced dewlap, although it is not as visible as that of a smooth-coated dog, on account of the dense, heavy coating around the neck and throat. The Tibet Mastiff's muzzle is somewhat longer, like that of the English Mastiff. His nostrils are well-expanded and open. His nose is well-developed, which shows clearly that the Tibet Mastiff would be capable of hunting, although this instinct, as a rule, is not promoted in his native homeland, since he is used there principally as a watch-dog. This extremely noble, aristocratic overall appearance distinguishes the Tibet Mastiff as a definite breed deserving promotion, cultivation and enhancement in Europe, in every possible way."

Partially quoting Youatt, the author Gordon Stables dismissed the Tibet Mastiff, without even picturing him, in the following words:

"One of the best specimens of this breed I ever saw in India or in Europe belonged to the Prince of Wales. This animal was named a Tibet Mastiff, yet he was more like a large, exceptionally unruly Newfoundland than anything else."

Vero Shaw does present a picture of the Tibet Mastiff with the following words, which, however, are partially repetitive of the above-quoted information:

"The Tibet Mastiff is actually, with regard to coat type and color, quite different from his English namesake, the English Mastiff; and, indeed, he does look more like a disgruntled, ill-tempered Newfoundland with incorrect ear-form than anything else. His head is short, broad and massive, his eyes deep-set, his lips are heavy and deeply sagging. All this together gives the dog a gloomy, unfriendly, fierce appearance, so that strangers are probably on their guard against approaching him. He has heavy bone, a very strong, powerful build and carries his tail raised up high and bent back over his back. His coat is long and harsh, not unlike that of a Newfoundland. The most frequent color is black with rust-red markings; all the individuals of better quality regarding type have fiery-red spots above the eyes, which stand out clearly.—Only a few representatives of this breed are found in England at all. One of the best of these was the dog named "Siring", owned by the Prince of Wales."

The picture published by Vero Shaw does not show the correct, genuine Tibet Mastiff type; it should be somewhere between the picture presented by Youatt and the one made by Hamilton Smith.

On page 216 of his book, the English author Stonehenge is equally brief:

"The Tibet Mastiff resembles the English Mastiff somewhat, and since he has the same duties to perform, both breeds may actually be distantly related. According to Mr. Bennett the Tibet Mastiff is bred and raised in the Himalayan Mountains, at Tibet's borders, in order to guard and protect the livestock herds and the women, who take care of and cherish him. Our illustration (copied from a picture by Youatt) renders a satisfactory mental image of the dog himself; his color is black, and his coat is rather long."

The French authors either quote the English authors, or else offer nothing that is really new about the Tibet Mastiff. The Frenchman Revoil wrote on page 116 of his book entitled *Historique Chiens (History of Dogs)* the following:

Due to his royal ownership, Siring was one of the most widely pictured examples of the breed. From *The Book of the Dog,* by Shaw.

"The Tibet Mastiff (Le Dogue du Tibet) is the most interesting and in appearance, the most representative, characteristic member of the Mastiff family.

"One must imagine how a massive Molossus looks, with a somewhat elongated muzzle, sagging lips, red-rimmed eyes deeply set in the bloodshot, uncovered conjunctivae, with long, straight, soft, raven-black coat as glossy as velvet. The Tibet Mastiff has densely coated hind-legs, which are 25 to 30 cm long, and a very bushy tail, which is 50 cm long and arched over his back. This is how the dog looks, which the Tibetans keep to guard their livestock. In Tibet, women and young girls are frequently the herders of the Yaks

97

and sheep. The overall appearance of this dog is savage and fierce: it is, indeed, terrifying."

Megnin, in his book entitled *Le Chien (The Dog)*, 2nd Edition, Vol. II, page 89, is not yet familiar with the Tibet Mastiff from first-hand observations; he finishes the Tibet Mastiff off very hurriedly in the following words:

"The Tibet Mastiff resembles both in size and appearance the English Mastiff. He is, however, long-coated with a heavily coated tail. His color in the upper body regions is red with black; in the lower body regions, his color is fawn and yellow. This breed became known mainly through the nice specimens that the Prince of Wales brought from India to England."

The Frenchman Gayot pictures the Tibet Mastiff in his book with plates; yet the illustration is miserable, indeed deplorable. He describes the Tibet Mastiff in the following words:

"We must not forget the Mastiff of Tibet. He has a strange appearance, more repugnant than friendly or trustworthy. His coat, which is long, black and rather rough, is unique and characteristic of this breed, just as the fur of all animals from those highland plateau regions. He has a high forehead, his drooping ears are narrow and small, lying flat. His eyes are half-covered by wrinkles, which makes him appear gloomy. His nose is large and fully developed. The overall appearance of this dog is neither friendly nor attractive, but rather dismal and terribly fierce. I do not believe that this breed is playful, nor trustworthy."

The Frenchman Jean Robert, in his book entitled *Le Chien d'Appartement et d'Utilite (The Dog of the Apartment and Utility Breeds)* repeats only that which was quoted above:

"The Tibet Mastiff has much that is analogous to the English Mastiff; he is, however, larger, more massive and stronger than the English Mastiff. His head is longer, his lips more sagging; and his overall expression is fiercer and more dismal. His eyes are bloodshot. His coat is long, also at the tail. His coat is much longer than that of the English Mastiff. In color, he is black with some yellow below the tail. His tail is held up like a flag, and it is arched over his back."

The French book *Le Chien*, which was written by an anonymous author and published by

R. H. Moore's drawing of Siring, who was exhibited at early shows.

Rothschild in Paris, does not forget the Tibet Mastiff:

> "This is the largest and strongest of all dogs. Generally speaking, this breed resembles the English Mastiff, yet he has more height at the withers and is more powerful and immense in body torso. The muzzle of the Tibet Mastiff is longer, the lips are quite sagging; the eyes are small and concealed in his head, but always surrounded by visibly bloodshot conjunctivae. The coat is long, somewhat rough, deep black; the hindquarters and tail are covered with long, soft coating. The tail is carried up high, arched back over his back.

> "The Tibet Mastiff's native homeland is the Himalayas, where he is bred by the people

of the high plateau or tableland. When the men climb down the mountains into the valleys and plains, in order to engage in trade, the dogs guard the women, who stay behind, at home. The traveler Marco Polo related that some of these dogs were as large as donkeys.[25] Others, who later traveled to Tibet[26] maintained that this was an exaggeration; but in the meantime, in fact quite recently, Marco Polo's descriptions have been found to be absolutely true.

"One finds the Tibet Mastiff already on the ancient sculptural relief of a pedestal from Niniveh, Assyria, which is now at the British Museum in London. Buffon wrote that he had seen a Tibet Mastiff that appeared to have a height of five feet while sitting.

"It is possible that dogs of this breed were transported into Macedonia and Epirus by Alexander the Great, where they became the famous "Molossus" dogs of the Greeks and Romans, being used there as fighting dogs in their circular gladiator arenas."

J. A. Petersen, who lived for many years in India, devoted the following chapter to the Tibet Mastiff in his book entitled *Uber Ostindische Hunde und ihre Verwendung zur Jagd (East In-*

dian Dogs and their Utliization as Hunting Dogs), which was published in St. Gallen, Switzerland, by the publisher Zollikofer:

> *"The Bhotea Mastiff or Tibet Mastiff:* The only really beautiful, nobly aristocratic dog breed of India is the Bhotea Mastiff or Tibet Mastiff. Apart from the Arabian dogs, the Persian dogs and the sight-hounds of the prairies and grasslands, which should be categorized together with the Borzois and Sloughis, considering their origin (Note: This is Petersen's own private view and opinion), the Tibet Mastiff is the nicest breed of entire Asia.
>
> "The Tibet Mastiffs are strong, large dogs of very typical, unique body anatomy, and thus cannot be confused with or mistaken for any other dog breed. The entire external appearance of the Tibet Mastiff signifies power and courage, coupled with a refined, distinguished bearing and a calm disposition, as could only be found among the mighty, who are aware of their power, dominance and superiority. The Tibet Mastiff's body is well-proportioned, his movements are uniform and beautiful in form. Characteristic is his head, which is extremely large, just as that of the English Mastiff, but is relatively wider

between the ears. The skull has a considerably developed occipital bone, because of which the ears of medium length, drooping down on both sides, appear to be attached at a lower point than they actually are. The muzzle is short and broad with a pronounced stop. The lips are deeply sagging and do not always completely close in the middle area, allowing the teeth to be seen somewhat. The bite itself is formidable, especially since the canine teeth are so well-developed. The mask has deep wrinkles, just as the English Bloodhound. The most pronounced wrinkle runs from the base of the muzzle toward the eyes; the other wrinkle runs from the muzzle base toward the nose. Wrinkles are also found above and below the deep-set, bloodshot eyes. All this gives the Tibet Mastiff a vicious, frightening appearance, in contrast with his friendly, innocent nut-brown eyes. His legs are powerful, well-proportioned, and his well-arched paws are closed. His tail is bushy, and it is carried arched over his back; this is so pronounced in some dogs that the tail can even rest on the highest part of the rump. The coat is long and rather rough; it has the greatest length under the neck and at the shoulders; at the hindquarters, the coat is often somewhat curled and wavy. The best color is black with tan markings, just as the color of the Gordon Setter or of the black-and-tan Manchester Terrier. However, pure black is also found sometimes, which must never have any white spots, patches or other markings. In addition, there are brown and dark wolf-gray individuals; the latter usually have black masks and black-tipped guard hair: these are considered to be less desirable, however. The strength of the Tibet Mastiff corresponds to his size. Unfortunately, I never got around to measuring one but it seems to me that the Tibet Mastiff (Bhotea Mastiff) is the giant, indeed the Goliath, among the dog breeds, beside which even English Mastiffs, St. Bernards and Newfoundlands would appear small, according to my mental picture of these breeds, although I have never had the opportunity of seeing these breeds standing together so that I could compare them.

"Next to his strength, the courage of the Tibet Mastiff is his main virtue, and he, upon his master's command, will ruthlessly and relentlessly attack the most formidable adversary or foe. Still, the Tibet Mastiff is very loyal and devoted to his master, extremely obedient and easy to manage.

"Bred almost exclusively by the natives of Tibet and in Bhotea (Bhutan), he is sometimes found as a luxury dog in the plains of India, but he does not tolerate the unhealthy climate there in the more humid lowlands very well. He soon becomes sickly and deteriorates. In his mountainous homeland, he is indispensable, and he is used there as a watch-dog and to protect the herds of sheep from the wolves, as well as to track down wolves.

"In India, two sub-species of wolves are found:

> 1.) The *Landagh* or, as he is called in central and northern India, the *Behria (Lupus pallipes)*: this wolf is grey in color and somewhat smaller than our Central European wolf. This small wolf is found, starting from the Himalayas, across all of western India.

> 2.) The *Chanko,* a considerably larger Tibetan wolf *(Lupus chanko):* this wolf, also grey in color, is found only in Tibet and the surrounding mountainous highlands. This wolf devastates the livestock herds of the natives there, causing severe losses, especially at-

tacking their sheep. Without the Bhotea Mastiffs (Tibet Mastiffs), it would be almost impossible to protect the sheep against the predatory inclinations of the marauding Chankos.

"Larger herds supervised by scarcely any shepherds are often seen under the care and protection of a few Tibet Mastiffs, and these loyal, courageous dogs not only keep exemplary order within the herds, guarding and defending these helpless animals the best they can against the wolves and other beasts of prey, but also violently attack these enemies and adversaries on their own initiative, which either attempt to flee, or they are killed by the Tibet Mastiffs.

"The Tibetan Mastiff is just as useful as a hunting dog. He will hold a huge Yak at bay, if this animal, wounded, plunges furiously at the hunter. He defends his master against any and all accidents or attacks that can befall him during hunting expeditions, which are there in the Himalayas, not always particularly free of risk and danger.

"As harsh and severe as these dogs are, in full consciousness of their great strength and their dreadful bites in resisting their en-

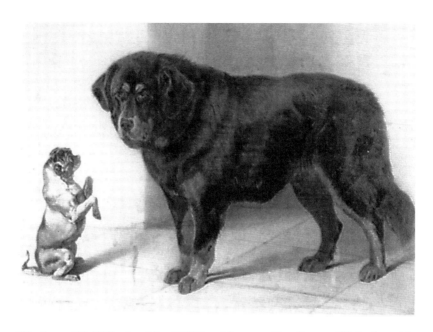

The beautiful Tibetan Mastiff "Bout," owned by Queen Victoria, with his Pug friend. This painting by renowned artist Friedrich Wilhelm Keyl is believed to date from 1850. *Collection Her Majesty the Queen.*

emies, they are equally as loyal and devoted to their masters. Truly touching is their affection and dedication to their master's family. It is as if they knew that they are the appointed guardians and protectors of the women and children. At planting and harvesting time, or when they go hunting, it can often occur that all the men leave their more or less neighboring farmsteads, and the women and children remain behind, now only under the protection of their loyal dogs. Entire villages from time to time have no protection from men at all, entrusted only to the guardianship and care of Tibet Mastiffs, who excellently fulfill their guard duties. These dogs would mercilessly rip any intruder to shreds who dared to even approach their protégés; whether this intruder be two-legged or four-legged would make no difference whatsoever.

"The Tibet Mastiff (Bhotea Mastiff) has many virtues and excellent qualities, but the best thing about him is his fine, upright character and good behavior. Unfortunately, this beautiful dog is rarely exported and brought into Europe, although he was already obtained along with wild animals, via land route from India, during antiquity by the ancient Greeks and Romans, who used him not only as a hunting dog, but also in the circular gladiator arenas as a fighting dog. At any rate, he would thrive here in the Nordic climate of northern and central Europe, since it is also very cold and bleak during the winter in his mountainous homeland, in spite of its southerly position on the map. I believe that the Tibet Mastiff could even be further ennobled and enhanced under the care, attention, guardianship and cultivation of serious breeders, especially within the Alpine climate of Switzerland or the mountainous regions of Germany. The transportation of these dogs from western

India on board one of the many English steamer lines, which have regular schedules, could be arranged and effected without great difficulty and at a reasonable price. If only a serious breeder would attempt to procure some good specimens of this worthy breed, he could, with certainty, look forward to great success within a short period of time. He would be promoting and cultivating a breed which would place many of our larger prestige and luxury breeds in the shade, even though the Tibet Mastiff is not especially apt as a hunting dog and too valuable to be used as a normal herding dog."

Ludwig Beckmann, the famous German animal artist, described the Tibet Mastiffs owned by Count Bela Szechenyi of Austria-Hungary in the *Leipziger Illustrierte Zeitung (the Illustrated Newspaper of Leipzig, Germany)* in the year 1880 as follows:

"The unique dogs of Tibet were usually depicted by early travelers, regarding their size and strength, in an exaggerated manner. The dogs owned by Count Szechenyi had approximately the size of larger German Pointers and reminded us to some degree, apart from their Mastiff-like profiles and tails rolled over their backs, of the smaller type of Newfoundlands known nowadays as the Dog of Labrador.

"The dense, long, supple coat lies smoothly and straight on the dog's body, with no signs of being curly or wavy whatsoever. The color is a lustrous deep black with yellowish-brown spots above the eyes and on the paws. The deeply wrinkled forehead, the small eyes with drooping corners and the deeply sagging lips gave Count Szechenyi's male a menacing expression, which did actually correspond to his rather vicious temperament. The female differed from the male only with regard to her smaller size and somewhat lighter body structure."

In his famous life's work, published in the year 1895, entitled *Die Rassen des Hundes (The Breeds of the Dog)*, Ludwig Beckmann dealt with the Tibet Mastiff longer and placed him, following the Great Dane and the large hound breeds of Spain and Denmark, into the same group with the St. Bernard and the Newfoundland. Beckmann wrote the following:

"The Dog of Tibet is the most Mastiff-like breed of this group, and could be called the Long-Coated Mastiff or the Tibet Mastiff, as the English named him. Even as early as the ancient Kingdom of Assyria, smooth-coated dogs existed which strikingly resembled the watch-dogs still bred at present in Tibet, except that the Dog of Tibet is long-coated. Of course, this ancient breed of Assyrian fighting dogs has long disappeared, just as the incomprehensibly cruel, inhuman folk of Assyria to whom this breed belonged. Only a few single pictorial representations of these Assyrian dogs have been found on pottery fragments in the ruins of Nineveh, Assyria. The breed itself was neither taken over and sustained by the Greeks nor by the Romans."

In further passages, Beckmann only repeats the information which we have already presented in our previous quotes from the publications by Bennett, Youatt, Turner and Dalziel. At the end of his section dealing with the Tibet Mastiff, Beckmann describes Cunningham's observations:

"Cunningham observed many Tibet Mastiffs in their native homeland. He described the tail carriage quite differently than most of the other writers, who have always described the tail as being turned back over the back in a pronounced arch. Cunningham considered it to be a definite breed characteristic that the tail bends so strongly and then lies

A magnificent study of a Tibetan Mastiff from Wood's *Animate Creation.*

so closely to the back that at the positions where the tail touches the back the coat is worn off short by constant friction. I made exactly the same observation when I examined two imported Tibet Mastiffs. Thus, I am convinced that there is considerable diversity among these dogs in this regard. Therefore, I would say that neither the pronounced rolling of the tail nor the looser arching of the tail can be fixed as *the* correct breed characteristic in the breed standard. Both variations should be equally accepted in the show ring."

Beckmann wrote further:

"Count Szechenyi's above-mentioned Tibet Mastiffs had been first taken to his country residence in Hungary, later to his castle at Neusiedler See in Austria. Besides the above-mentioned bending of the tail over the back, which reminded me in this regard of our German Spitz, I was surprised to notice the relatively small size of these dogs. Since even Hugh Dalziel, in his description of the Tibet Mastiffs owned by the Prince of Wales, noted that they did not attain the height of the English Mastiff, I consider the depictions of most of the travelers to be exaggerations with regard to the alleged "gigantic" size of the Tibet Mastiff. On the other hand, the dogs owned by Count Szechenyi fulfilled the utmost expectations with regard to watchful vigilance and protection against intruders, trespassers and thieves. Count Szechenyi's Tibet Mastiffs had approximately the height of larger German Pointers, but their rumps were more massive and they were lower in height at the withers, standing on short, straight legs. Their height would approximate that of the small variety of the St. Johns Newfoundland. In addition, their heads were larger and their necks were very densely coated, almost mane-like in appearance. On the rump, neck and tail, the coat appeared long, dense and hung down straight and smoothly, void of any signs of curling or waving. Below the belly and to the rear at the hindquarters, the longer coat feathered, but this feathering was almost absent, however, on the entire back side of the front legs. In addition, the hind legs were short-coated from the paws upward to within a hand's width of the hocks.

"The pronounced neck-mane terminated rather abruptly in the upper neck region near the head, and it formed below the throat a prominent, dense "coat beard", so that the entire head appeared rather short and densely coated. The numerous smaller wrinkles running diagonally on the broad forehead and the furrows or folds in the drooping lips and above the eyes were especially striking. The short ears, which did not lie particularly close to the head, were also short-coated. The small eyes of these dogs sparkled. But their entire facial expression was sullen and distrustful, not at all friendly. The muzzle was very short and blunt towards the front, with deeply sagging lips. As seen from the front, the muzzle region appeared to be rather narrow, as compared with the massive, broad, slightly arched (almost flat) upper head region. The color of the smooth, straight coat, which lay close to the body, was a deep, lustrous black with the well-known Dachshund-colored markings; however, these markings were of very limited dimensions. On the head there were only two tan-colored, round spots above the eyes and on the inner side of the front and rear legs. Only at the leg joints were there several small spots of the same color. The tail was relatively short. It was held either so firmly over the dog's back, drooping then down to the side, that the surrounding coat on the dog's back bristled up on both sides of the tail; or the tail, after loosely arching, drooped down straight and slack, already terminating then in the form of a blunt club, at the lower line of the belly. In spite of their short, straight, post-like legs and their small, round, massive paws, these dogs are said to be very swift and capable of making unbelievable high-jumps and broad-jumps. Without doubt, the Tibet Mastiff at first sight, with regard to most of his exterior details and characteristics, gives almost every dog enthusiast and expert the impression of being a definite, unique breed. The Tibet Mastiff occupies a unique middle-position somewhere between the appearance of Newfoundlands, English Mastiffs and the

Spanish Shepherd breeds. The vicious temperament of the Tibet Mastiffs, often emphasized by Europeans who had traveled to Tibet, could scarcely be inborn, but results simply from their early training and employment as watch-dogs in Tibet's half-civilized, sparsely populated regions."

Beckmann's article accompanied an excellent picture of Count Szechenyi's Tibet Mastiffs, both of which are somewhat Chow-Chow-like in type, which can also be seen from Beckmann's description quoted above. Since Count Szechenyi had reached Tibet from the side of Tibet bordering on China, purchasing his dogs near the Chinese border, it can be readily understood why Count Szechenyi's two specimens showed a certain tendency toward the Chow-Chow type. Beckmann presented, in addition, a drawing of the skull of a Tibet Mastiff; this drawing shows that the Tibet Mastiff's skull is more similar to that of a Newfoundland than to the skull of a St. Bernard. Beckmann's drawing of a St. Bernard skull is more English-Mastiff-like than that of the other two breeds, which have a less massive muzzle-portion. After observing the wide range of variability among the Tibet Mastiffs, I feel certain, however, that almost identical skulls of St. Bernards and Tibet Mastiffs could be found.

The Frenchman Pierre Megnin, in his book entitled *Le Chien et ses Races (The Dog and its Breeds)*, 4th Edition, Vol. I, which is one of the most accurate and best-written dog books now (1897) existing, regards the Tibet Mastiff as being identical to the ancient Assyrian Mastiff. In this regard, Megnin, Layard and I all share the same opinion. The Tibet Mastiff pictured by Megnin was taken from a photograph which he had obtained from the exotic animal dealer Jamrach in London. The dog was said to measure 90 cm (35.5 inches) at the withers; he was of a brownish-black color, with red markings. Megnin adds that the Tibet

Esteemed German artist and dog authority Ludwig Beckmann drew this portrait of "Dschandu" and "Dsama," owned by Count Belá Széchenyi.

Mastiff can also be found rather often in China, where the French missionaries use him to guard and protect their dwellings and in their settlements.

Professor Adolf Reul quotes in his excellent book entitled *Les Races de Chiens (The Breeds of Dogs)* mainly Megnin, the German author Brehm and the Englishman Samuel Turner: in other words he only repeats information that we have already presented. Noteworthy and somewhat surprising is Reul's following statement:

> "Travelers who have recently visited Tibet maintain that the Tibet Mastiff is not as fierce and courageous as one would normally think; and that, indeed, these qualities do not compare with his strength. Others report, however, that he only shows his courage against adversaries of equal strength. He is said to show particular antipathy and aversion towards Europeans, so that this is the main reason that he has been brought so rarely into Europe. This interpretation is not satisfactory, however, because Tibet Mastiffs raised by Europeans have repeatedly shown themselves to be not only very affectionate and devoted to their masters, but also extremely sociable and friendly."

The German zoologist Brehm presented in his famous animal encyclopedia entitled *Tierleben (Animal Life)* an excellent illustration of the Tibet Mastiff; in the wording of the text accompanying this illustration, however, little is offered which would be new for us. According to Brehm, the Dog of Tibet is a Mastiff which was already known by the Romans: a magnificent, beautiful and massive animal of truly awe-inspiring, respect-demanding appearance. The body and all its parts are strong and powerful; the tail, which is usually carried arched and over the back, is bushy. The ears are drooping. The lips do not always close at the front part of the mouth, and sag down deeply on both sides. A wrinkle, which originates from the external angle or corner of the mouth, extends to the front of the muzzle; this wrinkle is connected with another wrinkle, which slants diagonally downward from above the eye-brows. These wrinkles give the Tibet Mastiff's face a rather frightening appearance.

In the magazine *Chasse et Peche (Hunting and Fishing)*, which was published in Brussels, Belgium, Count Bylandt of Belgium wrote:

"The Tibet Mastiff is a definite, unique breed, which, neither to one side nor the other, could be regarded as a color or coat-length variety of one of the breeds with which we are already familiar here in Europe. Due to the fact that the Tibet Mastiff in his native homeland is almost the only domesticated animal, he is also utilized there as a working dog to guard and protect the Yak herds. We can only hope that this unique breed will soon appear at some of our dog shows here in Central Europe.

"The Tibet Mastiff is a large dog, yet he does not attain the height of the Great Dane. He is extremely powerful and of a typical, characteristic and unique body anatomy; thus, he cannot be mistaken for one of our European breeds. His body build documents power and courage, yet his behavior shows majestic dignity, as if he were conscious of his own power and superiority. His body is well-proportioned and beautiful in form. His head is the most distinctive feature: very large in circumference, just as massive as that of the English Mastiff, but with a somewhat longer muzzle and broader forehead between the ears.

"The skin of the forehead is wrinkled, as in the case of the St. Hubert Bloodhound; other wrinkles extend from the rim of the muzzle up to the area above the eyes. The occipital bone at the back of the skull is pronounced.

The ears are relatively small and drooping; and their point of attachment is located at a rather low position. The nose is short, and the inside of the nostrils is also black. The stops are very pronounced in this breed. The jaws of the Tibet Mastiffs are large and powerful; the mouth opens up wide. The lips sag deeply, and do not always completely cover the incisors. The bite is strong with well-developed teeth. Characteristic are also the Tibet Mastiff's eyes: because of the wrinkles surrounding the eyes, they have a fierce, melancholy expression, which, however, upon closer inspection is moderated and softened by the beautiful dark-brown eye color. The paws are well-arched and large; the straight legs are heavy-boned. The long coat, which is rather rough at the neck and throat, is frequently somewhat curly or wavy at the hindquarters (thigh region). The tail, which is of medium length and covered with long hair, is usually carried in an arch, bent back over the back. The color is black with rust-brown markings, just like the coloring of the Gordon Setter or a black-and-tan colored dachshund. Occasionally, solid black Tibet Mastiffs appear, which, however, should never have any white spots or patches. The height of the Tibet Mastiff at the withers is 70-75 cm (males) and 60-70 cm (females), or 27.5-29.5 inches (males) and 23.5-27.5 inches (females)."

At Crufts Dog Show in London, in the year 1896, one Dog of Tibet was entered. Count Bylandt, according to the magazine *Chasse et Peche* of Brussels, Belgium, had expected this dog to be a genuine Tibet Mastiff,

"Gyandru," owned by the great Tibetan dog fancier Mrs. Eric Bailey, in 1930. From *Hutchinson's Dog Encyclopedia.*

an animal with Keeshond coat-type and a head somewhere between that of a Chow-Chow and a Bloodhound. Instead, much to Count Bylandt's disappointment, only a so-called Dog of Tibet was entered: a reddish-yellow, shaggy, long-coated animal with a white chest and rather long, fine-boned legs—in type, a dog of the Russian plains, the Owtscharka. Obviously, the exhibitor himself did not know the breed of his own dog.

Travelers encountered in the regions surrounding Tibet and Bhutan, in the directions toward China, Upper Burma and Yuennan, only a very few Tibet Mastiffs, which, there in their new homes, were kept as something very special. It has been generally established that Tibet-Mastiff-like forms penetrate up into the north and into Chow-Chow-like dogs, or dogs related to the Chow-Chow. It is quite interesting to investigate and trace the intermediary steps between the Chow-Chow and the Tibet Mastiff, and to watch how these inter-mediate forms are gradually produced and trans-formed into each other, and then back into the extreme forms, the true Chow-Chow and the genu-ine Tibet Mastiff: in other words, how a broad-foreheaded, broad-muzzled, heavy-boned, large breed with drooping ears is developed, the higher we ascend into the Himalayan Mountains, out of a densely coated, dark-colored, finer-muzzled Chow-Chow. Professor Studer postulated a devel-opment of the Mastiff breeds from the Spitz breeds, to which the Chow-Chow belongs: in other words, the Mastiffs and Spitz breeds, according to Studer, would have the same ancestral progeni-tor. We also tend to support this theory, especially since having recently observed the similarity of heads in young Chow-Chows and St. Bernards. One could just as easily postulate, however, assuming that the two breeds had two different origins, that the links or intermediary forms between the Chow-Chow and Tibet Mastiff were produced by cross-breeding the two forms. Closer to Tibet, the dogs resemble the Tibet Mastiff more, because the he-reditary influences from the Tibet Mastiff are stronger; in addition, the adaptations with regard to geographical and climatic factors, over extremely long periods of time, would also play an important role. Approaching northern China, the native homeland of the Chow-Chow, the hereditary influences of this breed predominate in the intermediary forms found.

A special type of Tibet Mastiff, as has been documented, is found in Upper Burma, especially in northern and northeastern Burma, in the direction towards Tibet and China. Gill found Tibet Mastiff derivatives in the mountains adjoining the Tibet border in Chinese territory (30-33 degrees latitude, 104 degrees longitude), in the regions of San Pan Ting and Cheng Tu. He wrote the following:

> "The people of these regions keep very large, vicious dogs, which of all English breeds, would perhaps be most similar to a Collie. However, they have much more massive heads, stronger necks and broader fronts; their legs are quite short. One of these dogs had absolutely no intention of allowing us to enter the local inn at a village we were visiting."

Gill reports in his book entitled *The River of Golden Sand* that he had seen a purebred Tibet Mastiff in Sha Lu, near the Tibet-Burma border. He describes this dog in the following manner:

"The chief of the settlement in Sha Lu kept a mighty dog in a wooden cage at the wall beside the entrance-gate. This dog was a very massive animal, black with rust-brown markings. The brown-rust was of a very nice color. Brown-rust spots were located above the dog's eyes and on his chest The coat was rather long, but straight and smooth in texture. The tail was bushy; the legs were smooth, with rust-brown markings. His head was enormously large, downright unproportionate to the rest of his body; the head resembled that of a Bloodhound, with the overhanging, sagging lips and the deep-set eyes, clearly showing the bloodshot conjunctivae. His drooping ears were held flat, close to his head. He measured four feet from the tip of his nose to the root of his tail, and he was two feet ten inches height at the withers. This dog was three years old and of pure Tibetan breeding: a genuine purebred Tibet Mastiff."

Gill encountered further in Ta Tsien Lu (30 degrees 15 minutes latitude, 102 degrees longitude), which is located in the province Si Chuen, right on the Tibet border, very fierce black dogs, barking furiously with extremely deep-throated barks, when he entered a village homestead there. The heads of these dogs were similar to the heads of English Mastiffs with overhanging, sagging lips. They had bushy tails and long hair around the neck and throat.

Colonel Jule also reported about the dogs of this Chinese frontier borderland:

> "The mighty Tibet Mastiffs are probably known nowadays. Mr. Cooper reported from Ta Tsien Lu that the Tibetan tribes keep extremely large, strong dogs, which are as large as Newfoundlands."

He remembered further having observed a second Tibet Mastiff variety, black with rust-brown markings, which comprised a very noble kennel of dogs, which were the size of English Setters. In addition, the French missionary Durand reported in a letter from this region that his courageous watch-dogs had often repelled leopard attacks, but that in a fight with a huge leopard, one of his best dogs had received a terrible slashing blow from the leopard's fore-paw across the head, which had half-dissected his dog's skull.

The Austrian writer Kreitner, to whose excellent writings we have repeatedly made reference, also observed the gradual transition from intermediary Chow-Chow dog forms to Tibet Mastiff dog forms while approaching the Himalayas from the plains and foothills, on a trip from Si-ngan-fu to Lang-tschou-fu. He made the following obser-

Some found the Tibetan Mastiff to be affectionate, as this bitch clearly demonstrates.

vations about these transitional, intermediary forms:

> "While the dogs of China's southern provinces differ in appearance only slightly from that of a wolf,—indeed, at first, we had now and then mistaken them for wolves—the dogs in the province of Kan-su are almost pure breeds. Besides large, strong specimens, which appear, with regard to coat-type and body-structure, as if they were related to the Newfoundland, I also saw small, shaggy-coated dogs resembling Affenpinschers, as well as Dachshund-like dogs with dispropor-

tionately large heads. That the environment of this region exerted a favorable influence on dog vitality was demonstrated by the normal Chinese breeds there, which had thick, fat-storing tails, just as Mongolian sheep have."

From the foothills of the central Himalayas, J. B. Fraser also mentioned Tibet Mastiff derivatives:

"The breed of Bishur is famous for its size and courage. The best specimens that we saw were somewhat similar to English Mastiffs; nevertheless, they were not of pure Tibet Mastiff breeding. In Bishur, they were mostly black with white and some red markings. The coat was long and dense. The tail was long, bushy and densely coated, arched upwards, with the tip of the tail bent toward the back. The head was long, and in comparison with the English Mastiff, much narrower, resembling the head of a German Shepherd. Many of these dogs were very courageous and fierce. A few of them attained considerable size, yet only a very few attained the mighty size of a larger English Mastiff. All of these dogs there had a very fine-haired undercoat below their long, fluffy guardhair. In the warmer seasons, the undercoat is shed in flocks or tufts, along with some of the longer hair. All the animals here are protected by nature from the cold weather.[27] We observed that the natives use these dogs as shepherd-dogs in the same way this is done elsewhere, and further, however, to hunt game of all types, even birds, which they pursue until they tire from flying and are caught by the dogs.[28] Such dogs are extremely valuable."

From a neighboring region, the Gurwhal Mountains near the Puharies Mountains, the following is found in the book entitled *A Summer Ramble in the Himalayas*, which was published in the year 1860:

"In the lowest foothill regions, only mongrels are found, which are no better than the Pariahs of the plains. In the higher mountains, however, a more powerful, stronger breed exists, which originated in Tibet and is used there to guard the livestock herds. Two of these dogs suffice, at any time, to subdue a leopard; indeed, sometimes a single dog, one that is especially powerful and agile, is capable of mastering such a leopard. In spite of this, almost all of these dogs are killed sooner or later by the leopards, due to the fact that leopards often lurk, concealed in their well-chosen hiding places, and then suddenly jump down on the dogs, killing them in a surprising ambush before they have a chance to react."

This drawing appeared in the magazine Chasse et Peche (Hunting and Fishing),

J. N. Merk also encountered Tibet Mastiff derivatives in the foothills of the western Himalayas, not far from Rotang Pass, which leads into Chenab Valley. These were large dogs used for herding sheep, kept on account of the leopards. The dogs had long coats, narrower muzzles; and in appearance, they resembled bears. They were wearing broad collars made of iron, with spikes. Two of these dogs were a match for any leopard and were definitely capable of preventing one from attacking a herd of sheep.

In eastern Tibet, Rockhill encountered only a very few dogs accompanying the pastoral Drupa tribes of nomads, who have large herds of Yaks, horses, sheep and goats. Indeed, the Tibet Mastiff is extremely rare in eastern Tibet; on the other hand, Tibet Mastiff mongrels, in which the hereditary influence from the Tibet Mastiff is readily recognizable, are seen more frequently.[29] These make excellent watch-dogs.

At Lake Koko Nor, a Chinese salt lake, in the village of Baron, which lies 9880 feet above sea-level, Rockhill did not encounter a single Tibet Mastiff derivative, but only a few miserable mongrels, old women and a few men.

Prschewalski, the famous Russian explorer, took along two dogs from Saisson before entering northern Tibet during his last trip there. These dogs were not of pure breeding, but were, however, highly trainable for hunting purposes. Regarding these Tibet Mastiff mixes, Prschewalski reported the following:

> "These dogs' perceptive faculty was so remarkable that they were able to distinguish the sound of a shot-gun shot being fired at birds from the shot of a rifle fired at larger animals. After hearing the shot-gun fired, the dogs only pricked their ears, and just kept walking behind the caravan, where they were usually found. But as soon as they heard the sharp tone from a Berdan rifle, or even continuous firing from such rifles, they rushed forward immediately and pursued at highest speed the fleeing animals, the wounded ones of which they caught, as was often the case on antelope hunts."

In the interior of Tibet, the Tibet Mastiffs must be extremely valuable and highly esteemed, since they are often used there as sacrificial animals. During Prschewalski's trip to Tibet, two Tibetan Lamas or Buddhist monks joined him on the way; these two Lamas reported that the prospect of his arrival in Lhasa, in other words the arrival of a Russian, had caused great anxiety and agitation among the natives there; indeed, that the Dalai Lama had questioned shamanistic prophets and soothsayers, and that they had, with much ceremony and exorcism, killed a dog, hoping in great concern that, through such a sacrifice, potential harm or disaster might be warded off. In Tibet, as in China and Mexico, the same signs or symbols are used for chronological dating: one of these is the dog; others are, for example, the tiger and the monkey.

Hosie, who lived for a long period of time in the interior of China during the 1880s, was so fascinated by the dogs that accompanied Tibetan traders, which he had observed during his stay in western China, that he had made plans to acquire one of these dogs. Unfortunately, he was not able to fulfill this desire, because the dog brought over to him on trial was so wild and unruly that the entire strength of his strong, sturdy Tibetan owner was required to keep him under control. Had Hosie purchased this dog, which had been offered to him for 10 tails (Tibetan currency), he would also have had to engage the dog's owner as the care-taker.

Markham reported that it was impossible to go through the village's vigilant watch-dogs that then ran about loose. These were livestock-herding dogs, and they belonged to the same variety as the Dogs of Nepal; in other words, they were not purebred Tibet Mastiffs, but Tibet Mastiff derivatives or mixes. They were, however, very large dogs and both courageous and vicious toward strangers. They had longer mane-like coating at the neck, not unlike that of a lion, according to Markham. He reported that the folk of Pyn Cusho and of Rinzaitzog kept several kinds of dogs. One variety there, the Shamo, was especially treasured.

Moorcroft, in the year 1841, stated briefly that he had encountered large dogs in the provinces which lie within the foothills of the Himalayas. These dogs had long, rather rough coats, were black in color and scarcely tamer than the Purik sheep of this region.

Henderson and Hume, on their trip to Yarkand from Lahore, encountered not only in Ladak, but also *en route* with the nomadic Tibetan shepherds, a quite excellent, larger breed of dogs with long, rather rough coats. These dogs were, according to Henderson, not unlike Scottish sheep-dogs, except that they were much larger. They were very fierce and vicious, and were only kept in order to protect the livestock herds from wild animals. The enormous sheep herds owned by these Tibetans were always accompanied by some of these dogs. If a stranger approached the huts of these nomads, the women would rush out, then sit down on the dogs' heads and restrain them, until the traveler was far away again from their settlements. These dogs were difficult to obtain; in fact, for a good specimen, the Tibetans charged up to ten Pounds Sterling (in the 1880s). In the plains of India, they soon lost their beautiful long coats and usually did not survive even the second hot summer there. In England, Henderson had later found several excellent imported specimens of this breed, all of which had rendered excellent services as watch-dogs, guarding and protecting in an exemplary fashion their masters' property.

Just as the Tibet Mastiff sheds his dense coat when he is taken down into the hot, tropical low-lying plains of India, the same thing happens to the long-coated English breeds when they are imported into India. They degenerate within only a very short period of time with regard to strength, intelligence, coat-quality and overall health. They regenerate again, however, if they are taken up into the mountains and to Bhutan (Bhotea). After one or two months there, they acquire dense, fine, wooly undercoats and long, heavy guard hair, just as the native dogs possess there. The same thing applies to horses and other domesticated animals that are brought from the plains into the mountains. (Refer to *Journal Asiatique*, Vol. IX, published in the year 1826).

In closing, we must only go back to the earlier part of the 18th Century and finish up, using some of the earliest information ever published in Central Europe by Dr. Ludwig Reichenbach in his famous book entitled *Der Hund (The Dog)*, which appeared in the year 1836. His report depicting the Tibet Mastiff contained three relatively good color pictures. He wrote the following:

> "Even Strabo, the famous Greek geographer of the first century B.C. and the early first century A.D., mentioned the excellent Dogs of India, as well as Aelian *(in Hist. Anim. 19)* and Marco Polo. At the beginning of the 1830s in this century, these dogs were accurately introduced to England's dog enthusiasts, in that Thomas Landseer painted one of these dogs in the year 1830, and William Harvey described this dog. Dr. Wallich, Professor of Botany in Calcutta, India, imported at that time, as a matter of fact, some of these dogs into England. He, at the same time, presented the following information:
>
> > 'These dogs come from the high plateaus of the Himalayan Mountains, from the region now known as Tibet. Their masters are the Bhoteas, to

whom these dogs are completely devoted. These dogs show an irreconcilable antipathy and aversion toward Europeans; indeed, they generally retreat furiously at the first glance of a Europeans white-skinned face. A warmer climate reduces all their strength; and even in the Valley of Nepal, they deteriorate and become weak and sickly. The specimens imported into England around the year 1830 were of a very fine, noble breed type; they were derived from the vicinity of Diggarschee, the capital of Tibet. They are probably the first that had ever been tamed by Europeans. The British Consul at the palace of the Rajah of Nepal and Katmandu, Edward Gardener, had never heard of any other importations of this breed into England; and he, therefore, regards these particular purebred Tibet Mastiffs as extreme rarities. Unfortunately, they died soon after their arrival in England.'"

They did not survive, presumably, because they were unwisely kept confined in cages, without enough space and exercise at London's Tower Menagerie.

This poor quality drawing is included here for its historical significance. This is a TM imported to London by the exotic animal dealer Jamrach, who lived in Paris. Jamrach imported about a dozen TMs, all undersized. Some went to Berlin and the rest went to London. Only one or two were said to be typical specimens. This drawing came from the Belgian magazine *Chasse et Peche* and was copied from a drawing which appeared in *Les Races des Chiens*, by famous French authority Pierre Mégnin.

Captain Rapes, in his story about the expedition leading to the discovery of the Ganges River, also mentioned that the inhabitants of Bhutan had brought large dogs to market for sale, as part of their merchandise. He described one as being a very beautiful animal, as large as a larger Newfoundland, heavily coated with long hair, and of the appearance of a Bull-Biter (Molossus). His tail was of considerable length, like a fox-tail, and arched upwards over his back. He was, moreover, so vicious that he would not let strangers come near him. Captain Rapes reported that this same self-willed obstinacy had also been observed in other specimens of this breed.

In addition to this, Mr. Moorcroft reported, upon his return from Lake Manasa-Sarovara, that the Uniyas were accompanied by dogs which were very fierce and which were extremely inclined to attack strangers. Mr. Traser, who described his trip to the Himalayas, often mentioned the Dogs of Bischur, whose strength, power and agility he described in an interesting fashion. He was the only person, however, who ever said that Tibet Mastiffs were *not* more massive than German Pointers, which shows clearly that he had never seen the genuine Tibet Mastiff. (As already noted above, the Dogs of Bischur are only mongrelized derivatives of the genuine Tibet Mastiff, produced by crossbreeding.)

The Tibet Mastiffs exhibited in London's Tower Menagerie were larger than any English Mastiff that had ever been seen. The color of these

A curious photo of a "Russian Mastiff." It does not reveal any current Russian breed. Despite the short coat, some have felt that this dog bears a resemblance to the Tibetan Mastiff and may have carried some TM blood.

Tibet Mastiffs was deep black, but at the sides slightly grey. Their paws and a spot above each eye were a deep rust-red color or light brown. They had a broad, blunt muzzle like that of a Bull-Biter (Molossus), and their lips sagged even more than that of the Molossus. One noticed, indeed, a unique coat flaccidity, which Desmarest designated as being a specific breed characteristic of the breed he named the "Tibetan Bull-Biter", without going on to further describe this breed.

Tibetan Mastiff

A lovely drawing of a pair of Tibetan Mastiffs. *From Hutchinson's Dog Encyclopedia.*

Chapter Five

Personal Observations and Conclusions

During our own travels throughout English India, we had hoped to see far more Tibet Mastiffs and to hear much more about them than was actually the case. Even English dog enthusiasts and fanciers, with whom we spoke there, only knew of this breed's existence, but very little about the breed itself or where exactly these dogs could actually be found. Even at the museum in Calcutta, within their copious zoological collections, in which even skillfully stuffed dogs were displayed, which the taxidermist Hodgson had collected in Nepal and Bhutan, the Tibet Mastiff was totally missing; not even a Tibet Mastiff skull could be shown us at that time (in the year 1888).

It was clear to us that in the lower-lying plains of India, few or no Tibet Mastiffs could be bred, because they cannot thrive in the hot climate there, although imported St. Bernards are seen now and then in Calcutta. The Tibet Mastiff simply cannot withstand the tropical climate and pollution there.

It struck me as strange, however, that in the hill regions and in the Himalayan foothills, up to an altitude of 10,000 feet, where Europeans have settled and manage tea plantations, only very few Tibet Mastiffs are found. The reason for the rarity of this breed in the regions of India colonized by Europeans is, no doubt, their fierce, uncivilized behaviour acquired at an early age from their native masters, from whom they learn to hate everything that is foreign, and the fact that the Europeans in India are not interested in anything other than having ordinary mongrel watch-dogs requiring a minimum of investment, of time and of care. Another reason that this breed is seldom found outside of its native homeland is that Europeans rarely stay long enough in these regions to do any serious breeding of Tibet Mastiffs, which would lead to their having better temperaments and to their being friendlier to Europeans. There is no doubt at all that this noble breed could soon be promoted by dedicated breeders, engaged in improving and cultivating the breed, to a developmental niveau approximating that of our present European breeds. Indeed, an extremely engaged dog fanatic or a real dog expert would be necessary and requisite to train and keep a dog of the type that is sold to Europeans by the natives of this region as a mature, adult animal. Just imagine trying to keep a dog of St. Bernard size, but with much greater strength and agility, which is as

The famous "Tonya," born in 1933. Her photo appeared in many books as a typical illustration of the breed.

unruly as a wild animal, in your house. It has been observed in a few cases here in Europe that St. Bernards which were not trained or socialized at an early age could also be almost as vicious as wild animals, although such dogs were usually, in such cases, more prone to direct their aggressiveness toward other dogs than toward human-beings. We wish to remind our readers of the behaviour sometimes shown by St. Bernard males from large kennels. Our readers are just to imagine how much more ferocious and dangerous a Tibet Mastiff would be that was raised by an uncultured folk and intentionally trained to be vicious toward strangers.

A Tibet Mastiff raised from puppyhood by Europeans is, of course, friendly to white people. Our innkeeper in Darjeeling was a German-Austrian. (Darjeeling is in India, 300 miles north of Calcutta.) He owned a beautiful Tibet Mastiff, but this dog was, as a European's dog, hostile to the dark-skinned natives there. Our innkeeper only released that strong, powerful Tibet Mastiff from his kennel under great precautionary measures, because he had an excessive aversion against dark-skinned people, a strong predilection and inclination for the bare, thin legs of the black-skinned natives of the low-lying plains!

A mature Tibet Mastiff in and around Darjeeling, which lies in India's northern West Bengal, in the Himalayan foothills, was worth at that time (in the year 1888) 100 to 200 rupees, but for this price one would only get a Tibet Mastiff of mediocre, third-rate breeding quality. Splendid, first-rate specimens are rare, just as in any other breed, unless one is dealing with a serious breeder. These mediocre dogs predominated, but they did show, however, in all their characteristics, definite signs of representing a distinct, unique breed-type, which could have been intensified and molded into genuine breed characteristics through selective breeding. In recent years, a false opinion about the Tibet Mastiff has been formed in many cases; this false conception is based on the very few Tibet Mastiffs which have been seen in Europe during the last 10 to 20 years. To confirm this, we must only make reference to the information from the different sources quoted in previous chapters.

Regarding the best representatives of the breed,

In 1934, Mrs. Bailey imported Drenjong Dakpa.

the Tibet Mastiff does not fall short of the best comparable European breeds, such as the St. Bernard, Newfoundland and English Mastiff, with reference to size, strength, power, heaviness of bone, coat density, color and overall beauty. But so-called top specimens of the breed that are of absolutely top show quality are very rare, as in all breeds. In the hands of serious, conscientious breeders, the Tibet Mastiff could be improved very rapidly, not only with regard to external characteristics, but also with a view to temperament and disposition. Let us take a look at the English Mastiff and the St. Bernard as breeds comparable to the Tibet Mastiff. From the years 1800-1860 there were some representatives of these two European breeds measuring up to 80 cm (31.5 inches), but these were extremely rare, because they had appeared at random, accidentally, and not as a result of careful selective breeding. When we ourselves began our carefully planned program of breeding St. Bernards for the show ring back in 1880, we had difficulty in finding a quality male that would measure 76 cm (30 inches) at the withers at maturity. The best male that we were able to purchase at that time attained only 70 cm (27.5 inches) after reaching maturity, and our foundation female only attained 60 cm (23.5 inches). Now, only seventeen years later, a height of 76 cm (30 inches) for a female is nothing out of the ordinary, and a male measuring 80 cm (31.5 inches) is even considered right small. Such extremely rapid size changes can be observed within a breed as soon as selective breeding methods are established and employed, aided by scientifically balanced nutrition. This would also apply to the Tibet Mastiff. In the year 1892, a Tibet Mastiff set a record as being the largest dog in England; in 1815, it had been a St. Bernard. Co-existing with these exceptional giants that had appeared by chance, the breed's smaller, original type still existed and continues to exist, of course. Through selective breeding, these smaller original forms could be transformed into the size of the larger exceptions.

Let us now make a summary of all the presented information concerning the Tibet Mastiff:

1.) We are indebted to the Chinese for the oldest reports dealing with the Tibet Mastiff. These reports date back to 1100 B.C.

2.) The oldest pictures of a breed resembling the Tibet Mastiff were made by the Assyrians. Although these pictures were not discovered until modern times, they can be traced back to the period around 700 B.C.

3.) From the 4th Century B.C. onwards, Greek and Roman historians, enlightened mainly by the knowledge of Central Asia obtained by Alexander the Great's military expedition into India, mention the Dogs of India, which can be called Tibet Mastiffs. These Greek and Roman historians were, for example, Ktesias, Aristotle, Megasthenes; then later Strabo, Herodotus, Aelian, Curtius and Gratius Faliscus.

4.) From ancient India itself, only one possible picture from the 3rd Century B.C. has been discovered. In the old Sanskrit literature of India, "four-eyed"

A dog imported in 1906 by the Prince of Wales. On the journey to England, on the Red Sea, those attending the dog thought he was suffering unduly from the heat. Therefore, they shaved him. When he arrived in London, he was housed at the Zoological Gardens. Unfortunately, he was placed in a cage exposed constantly to the summer sun. He died within a few months. His shorn coat makes it possible for us to observe the similarities between the Tibetan Mastiff and the English Mastiff. From *The New Book of the Dog.*

vicious dogs are mentioned: in other words, black-and-tan dogs with a tan spot above each eye. These dogs could easily have been the ancestors of the Tibet Mastiff known today.

5.) Around the year 1300, the Venetian Marco Polo became acquainted with the Tibet Mastiff.

6.) Not until the 18th Century were Tibet Mastiffs accurately described by

Europeans who had discovered them as imported dogs in their own home countries. Samuel Turner is due great honor for being the first who ever brought accurate reports of this breed from this travels back to Europe, where the Tibet Mastiff was still completely unknown.

7.) Good, authentic reports after those of Samuel Turner were presented around the year 1830 by Hodgson, Dr. Wallich and Hooker, then later by Kreitner.

8.) Except for brief statements, almost all the information about the Tibet Mastiff later presented by travelers, for example Cunningham and Henderson, was not taken from their own personal, first-hand observations, but was plagiarized from the original material which had already been presented around 1830. This explains the great conformity in all later reports. These authors all copied from each other. Most of them plagiarized Youatt, for whom, in turn, friends had compiled all the source information he actually indirectly presented.

The size of the Tibet Mastiff corresponds to that of the English Mastiff, the St. Bernard and the Newfoundland. It varies between 70 and 90 cm (27.5 and 35.5 inches) for dogs, and from 60 to 80 cm (23.5 to 31.5 inches) for bitches: this is the height measured at the withers. The average height is between 70 and 75 cm (or 27.5 to 29.5 inches), just as it is for the three other comparable larger breeds. The weight in their native homeland Tibet is seldom 100 kilograms (220 pounds), since these dogs are not scientifically fed there, as we do here in Europe with our English Mastiff, St. Bernard and Newfoundland show dogs. In Tibet, these dogs are active, hard-working utility dogs. Here in Central Europe, the Tibet Mastiff will probably have an average weight of around 220 to 265 pounds.[30]

The Tibet Mastiff's head is for dog experts the most important body part. It is an intermediate somewhere between an average, broad-foreheaded, rather broad-muzzled Great Dane head and a massive Bloodhound or English Mastiff head. Too much head-skin with extremely large furrows, lips too long and extremely sagging eye-lids can sometimes be found, just as in the best St. Bernard breeding programs of former years.

The ears are always overhanging and drooping, usually set high and wide apart, but not very long and should lie close to the head. They also vary, however, in length, size and how much

The impressive "Bhotean" was obtained by Major Dougall during the last Youngblood Expedition, to Lhasa, Tibet, in 1904. He was considered, by many Tibetans, to be an especially fine specimen. Dougall characterized him as a devoted "one man's dog." He was kind to all women and children and perfectly safe with them. However, he hated all men on sight. This made the journey to England quite difficult. On his trip through India, he had to have his own carriage. In 1906, Dougall showed Bhotean at the Crystal Palace show. It was the custom to put prices on the dogs and allow them to be "claimed" by remitting the amount. Dougall put a very high price on his rare dog. To his surprise, Bhotean was purchased by Sir William Ingram. From *The New Book of the Dog*.

they droop, just as they vary in the St. Bernard. The eyes should always be dark brown, but occasionally they may be lighter in solid dark-colored dogs, due to a color degeneration, which should be regarded as a fault. Many have eye-lids that close completely; others show the inner side of the lower eye-lids, as well as the bloodshot conjunctivae. These, also having many pronounced wrinkles on the head, which form angular furrows, are the ones preferred in the show ring. Dewclaws, either simple or double, are, just as in the case of the St. Bernard, to be regarded

A 1904 photo of "Dsamu," owned by Mr. H. C. Brooke, a great fan of rare breeds.

as distinct breed characteristics. Their development resulted from adaptation to the terrain (snow and ice), which the Tibet Mastiff must traverse each year. Just as in the case of the certain few St. Bernard lines known to have some English Mastiff ancestry in their distant bloodlines and in which lines the dewclaws are almost invariably missing, these dewclaws can also be missing in some of the Tibet Mastiff lines, probably those that were partially derived from Tibet Mastiff breeding stock having some crossbreeding with the Pariah dogs of India's plains in their distant ancestry, even though this is no longer otherwise recognizable in their external appearance. As with the St. Bernard, foreleg dewclaws appear only sporadically.

The color of the Tibet Mastiff is black with yellow, rust-brown or red markings, just as we see them on the Gordon Setter, the black-and-tan Manchester Terrier and the black-and-tan Dachshunds. Sometimes these markings are larger or more extended, sometimes smaller or in more limited extension; sometimes they are bright, sometimes they tend to be drab in color; on a few individuals they are almost completely missing. Nevertheless, they are never totally missing, as for example in the Newfoundland, in which breed the specimens with markings are the rarest. In most breeds that have the black-and-tan color pattern, solid reds are also found. This color is, in the case of the Tibet Mastiff, usually more of a light brown, called "yellow" or "gold", and is only found relatively seldom. Red with a black saddle is found more often than solid red. In addition, yet very rarely, blue (a slate gray color) specimens with red markings have appeared.[31] Extensive white markings on Tibet Mastiffs are never found; even tiny white spots on the chest or toes are extremely rare.

The coat can vary in length and density somewhat; nevertheless, it must still be clearly classifiable as long, by all means. Underneath the longer, often very long straight guard hair, which is sometimes rather silky in texture, sometimes quite coarse, lies a short, soft undercoat. Many specimens could be called "shorter long-coated dogs"; others have, at least at the neck, a relatively profuse coat resembling a mane; others have a profuse coat distributed over the entire body, except for the extremities. The head, the ears and the legs have short hair. However, the tail is long-coated. Corresponding to the season of the year, the coating can also vary.

The tail is never carried in a Pointer-bird-dog-like manner, but either bent well over the back in a pronounced arch or bow, so that the tip of the tail touches the back; or the tail is curled or rolled, whereby it usually rests on the left thigh. The unrolled, simple arching of the tail over the back is perhaps the preferable form, since those with rolled tails probably have more ancestral hereditary influence from the Chow-Chow in their distant bloodlines. When the dog is resting, the tail can hang down. It is bushy and very long-coated. On the back, the long coat bristles up on both sides next to the tail at the location where the tail rests on the dog's back; and in the region where the tail bends over the back, the long coat can be worn away to appear short.

The leg bones are heavy and round in form, rather stubby, but should not be so extremely heavy and short that they appear clumsy or awkward, as has sometimes been seen here in European show rings. The thighs at the hindquarters are rather flat, a peculiarity of the Tibet Mastiff which is actually a natural characteristic for breeds which were developed in mountainous regions. The breed's tendency to be rather straight stifled and slightly cow-hocked is also characteristic.[32] The paws are small, well-closed and arched; and they are usually densely coated.

The bark is deep-voiced and resonant, corresponding to that of our other larger breeds.

The bite is strong and well-developed; the yawning abyss and throat are wide open. The lips are very pronounced, sagging deeply. In some specimens, however, the lips may sag less, close more completely and cover the bite completely.

Shekar Gyandru with a puppy from the first litter born in England, in 1931. The dogs were owned by Mrs. Eric Bailey who did so much to spur interest in all the Tibetan breeds. From *Hutchinson's Dog Encyclopedia*.

"Tomtru," imported to England, won at many shows in the 1930s.
From *Hutchinson's Dog Encyclopedia.*

In many individuals, the head is very wrinkled, the skin there forming diagonal wrinkles from the eyes to the corner of the mouth. Other specimens, however, may show nothing unusual in this regard. The head-skin appears to be somewhat too loose for the skull.

The muzzle is usually long and relatively narrow in the specimens having a high, arched upper skull region and a pronounced occipital bone at the rear part of the skull. Others possessing more of a flat upper skull usually have simultaneously a rather short, blunt, broad muzzle with lips that are too long.

Lower jaws that are too short appear less frequently in the Tibet Mastiff than in the modern type of English Mastiff or St. Bernard.

In all Tibet Mastiffs, the head and muzzle are clearly set off and separated by a pronounced stop that forms an angle approaching 90 degrees.

The back is rather short; leggy specimens are undesirable, and fortunately appear only rarely.

The overall impression made by the Tibet Mastiff is that of a powerful, strong, large, but yet agile and active dog that is never ungainly, awkward or clumsy. The free, unbridled, rugged life and strong natural selection prevented the emergence of any degenerative tendencies which would have resulted in a lack of physical coordination or body fitness.

The color of the markings, as well as the size and extent of the markings, determine how sullen, menacing and vicious the Tibet Mastiff may appear. As a rule, his appearance is not very friendly or amiable, but impressive and majestic. A dog enthusiast will invariably approach him, at first at any rate, with caution.

The main duties in his native homeland are those of a watch-dog, to protect the villages there against unexpected attacks, to defend the livestock herds against beasts of prey, which are mainly leopards, wolves, bears and smaller predatory animals. He also serves as a pack animal. In the modern sense, the Tibet Mastiff is not a real herding dog like a German Shepherd or the British sheep-dog varieties, since he is not sufficiently specialized through domestication. He is not a real hunting dog, either: he hunts, if occasion arises, from natural instinct, not on account of extremely specialized sensory organs developed through human selective breeding, such as those found, for example, in bird dogs and scent hounds. The development of a real shepherd or sheep-dog breed in the modern European sense, or the development of a genuinely trainable hunting breed, would have demanded a far higher human cultural level than that which was possessed by the Peptschas, Bhotias, Tibetans and the nomads of Nepal.

Jumla's Kalu of Jumla, owned by Ann Rohrer, pictured at ten years of age. This dog, who battled a snow leopard, was imported to this country in 1970. The exciting story of Kalu's life is told in *The Tibetan Mastiff, Legendary Guardian of the Himalayas,* by Ann Rohrer and Cathy J. Flamholtz, OTR Publications.

The Tibet Mastiff has a certain value as an article of export to certain provinces outside of his native homeland, mainly those which lie to the east or north (for example, in China). There he serves less as a watch-dog, but is kept there more as a curiosity, even in cages, not unlike a menagerie animal.

The Tibet Mastiff will, no doubt, sooner or later attain a wide range of distribution throughout Europe. Tibet is becoming more and more accessible. Bhutan can already be reached rather easily.

A trip from Europe to Tibet takes much less time nowadays (1897); thus, it is becoming easier and easier to overcome the greatest obstacle that previously had blocked the export of Tibet Mastiffs; arranging and managing their transport from the mountains of Central Asia through the plains of India and over the hot sea into the cool climate of northwestern Europe.

In the foreseeable, if not immediate future, we shall find the Tibet Mastiff at all our dog shows. It will take only a few generations to make a watch-dog, companion-dog and impressive luxury-dog out of him, at least in the majority of the specimens bred, which would be suited to and fit for our western civilization. The many characteristics that he has in common with the St. Bernard, our Dog of the Swiss Alps, will enable him to thrive in our climate.

Chapter Six

The Standard

GENERAL APPEARANCE:

Large, powerful, imposing, majestic and impressive; a unique breed; in size, not smaller than Newfoundlands, St. Bernards and English Mastiffs. This dog expresses power and courage in his bearing and demeanor, without appearing cumbersome or awkward. The appearance is more grim, stern and earnest than friendly, amiable or good-natured. The entire body is well-proportioned. The legs are not too long, but the body not extremely deep. In spite of his size and strength, the dog appears agile.

HEAD:

The head is the most powerful, characteristic part of the body. As large as possible, massive and rather long in the muzzle region. The upper head region is broad, but the skull is usually arched somewhat more than that of the English Mastiff and St. Bernard. The occiput is usually visible. The muzzle is not too broad, rather long, but very deep. A strong, pronounced stop is clearly noticeable. The dark brown, deep-set eyes are not especially large. The eyes show the conjunctivae and form frequently in the lower eye-lid a cornered fold. The lips should be strongly developed and cover the teeth. Large wrinkles should be present behind the eyes, running toward the corner of the mouth, and on the forehead. The yawning abyss and throat should open widely. The mucous membranes of the oral cavity should be dark in color. The nose must be black in color. The bite should be sound and very strong.

EARS:

The ears should be rather high set and wide apart, neither furrowed nor wrinkled. They should lie close to the cheeks. The ears should be V-shaped (triangular), not particularly large and smooth-coated (short-haired).

NECK:

The neck should be short and strong. The neck appears shorter, compacter and more bull-necked than it actually is, due to the mane-like, lengthened hair around the neck.

BODY:

The body is powerful, lies rather deeply between the forelegs and is barrel-shaped at the chest. The back is broad and straight. The hindquarters are not very muscular, tending to be only very slightly angulated at the hocks and thus somewhat straight-stifled. Many tend toward the very cobby, compact build of the Spitz breeds. The legs should be rather short, strong, straight and rounded. The legs should not be excessively heavy-boned, and they should appear, in relationship to the massive body, rather short.

PAWS:

The paws should be small, round and well-closed. They should not be too heavily coated between the toes. Dewclaws, not only simple (single), but also double dewclaws, may be found on the inside of the hind legs. The fifth toe (dewclaw) may occasionally be found on the forelegs.

TAIL:

The tail is rather short and bushy-coated. It is either bent straight back over and toward the back in a pronounced arch, so that it touches the middle of the back with the blunt tail-tip, without turning to the right or left; or, soon after being bent over, it lies in a roll to the left or to the right on the croup and hindquarters.

COAT:

The Tibet Mastiff should have a soft, wooly undercoat. The guard hair should be straight, and it may vary in texture from silken to coarse. The coat is the most profuse at the neck and tail. The straight guard hair may vary from a harsh, stand-off texture, as in the Spitz breeds, to a more silky texture. The head, ears and legs should be covered with smoother, shorter hair. At the thighs ("trousers"), on the back and around the neck, the coat is the longest.

COLOR:

The most frequent color is black with rust-brown markings (as in the black-and-tan Dachshund, black-and-tan Manchester Terrier and Gordon Setter), whereby the rust-colored markings may vary from yellowish to dark mahogany. Solid red, red with a dark saddle, almost solid dark black-brown and brown-and-tan are also found. White may only appear as a small spot on the chest or toes.

HEIGHT AT THE WITHERS:

70 - 90 cm (27.5 - 35.5 inches) for dogs; 65 - 80 cm (25.5 - 31.5 inches) for bitches.

WEIGHT:

107 - 215 pounds.

ORIGIN:

Eastern Himalayan Mountains, Bhutan, Sikkim and Tibet.

POINT SCALE FOR JUDGING THE TIBET
MASTIFF IN THE SHOW RING:
(by Count Bylandt of Belgium around the year
1893)

General Appearance:	10 Points
Head	10 Points
Wrinkles	15 Points
Ears	5 Points
Eyes	5 Points
Body	10 Points
Paws	10 Points
Tail	15 Points
Coat	10 Points
Color	10 Points
TOTAL	100 Points

Footnotes

1. The *Mastin* was described by Franz Krichler and pictured in the newspaper *St. Gallner Centralblatt,* Vol. VIII, in 1892.

2. Refer to the publications of B. Siegmund and Professor Theodor Studer found in the Schweizer Hundestammbuch (Swiss Dog Registry Book Vol. II and III and V; publishers: Verlag von Orell-Füssli, Zürich, Switzerland, and Zollikofer in St. Gallen, Switzerland).

3. Pierre Mégnin, the well-known French scholar on canine development, postulates the following primitive forms of the domesticated dog:

> a. The European Stone Age Torfhund, Dog of the Peat Bogs: *Canis familiaris palustris,* Dog of the Stone Age Lake Dwellers, described by Professor Rütimeyer of Basel, Switzerland.

b. A huge, genuine Molossus-like dog, which the Aryans of Asia later brought to Europe.

c. A very large Greyhound-like sight-hound from Africa, already owned and pictured by the ancient Egyptians and which is still today the most ferocious dog in Kordofan (central Sudan).

We differ from Mégnin inasmuch as we assume that the St. Bernard could have developed during the course of time from the primitive Stone Age dog of the Peat Bogs *(Canis familiaris palustris)*, in accordance with the publications of B. Siegmund, Swiss Dog Registry Book, Volume V. We believe that the Tibet Mastiff could also have developed from *Asiatic* forms of this primitive Lake Dwellers' Stone Age Dog of the Peat Bogs, since, according to Professor Theodor Studer (Swiss Dog Registry, Vol. III), fossil remains of this particular Stone Age dog have also been found there in Asia. Mégnin postulated a separation of the *paulstris* dogs and the heavy Molossus-type dogs. This postulation was based on Professor Nehring's theory that a prehistorical *Canis familiaris decumanus,* which was a heavy Molossus-like dog, co-existed with *Canis familiaris palustris* during the same period of the Stone Age.

4. Col. Hamilton Smith, for example, formulates the hypothesis, which, in any case, is difficult to prove, that all our Mastiffs, or as the case may be, Mastiff-like dogs, were derived from the colder regions of Central Asia; they reached Europe with the mass Stone Age migrations, and later they were brought to England by the Celtic Cimbrian tribes.

5. Pierre Mégnin believes, on the basis of the following evidence, that we may assume that all the Molossus breeds are of Asiatic origin:

> "During Alexander the Great's march to India, he, at the Indus River, was shown gigantic Molossus-type dogs, which were trained to fight with lions and elephants. Through Alexander the Great's conquest marches to Asia, this dog was brought to Europe, first of all to Macedonia, where he was soon named the 'Molossus' after the city of Molossus in the ancient Grecian state of Epirus. From there the Romans engaged him in fights within the circular gladiator arenas. From Italy the Romans brought him to Great Britain, where he especially thrived. From here he later reached Gaul and Germania. The name *Alan,* which he was given by the inhabitants of Gaul and which he kept up until the Middle Ages, is surely of Celtic origin, because this word does not exist in

the Latin language, yet it has been preserved up to the present time in Italian, as seen in the Italian name *Alano* for their massive Molossus-type dog." (P. M. L'Eleveur)

Further, the Asiatic tribes migrating to the west kept huge, powerful dogs for protection, to guard their tents and campsites and to aid them in battle. This was well-documented by the Celtic Cimbrian tribes, the Teutons, the Huns, etc. It is very probable that the present-day Tibet Mastiff is at least a partial remnant of the Molossus of antiquity which Columella, a contemporary of Virgil, described in the following manner:

> "very massive and heavy, with a deep-voiced bark, which terrifies thieves and villains; of dark color; compact in build, neither too long nor short, with an enormous head, which seems to be the largest part of the body; the flop-ears lightly folded; the eyes dark or even gleaming with a greenish tinge. Chest broad and well-coated. Shoulders broad, hind legs and thighs strong with rough coat; large paws with strong claws." (L'Eleveur, in 1891)

This description of Columella's fits the Tibet Mastiff, aside from his description of the ears, because, for the Romans, the type shown in the picture on page 49 was the Roman's idealized conception of the Molossus, in other words, their standard. Strangely enough, there is no dog picture from ancient Greece or Rome, as far as we know, which renders a genuine Molossus as portrayed in the Assyrian picture (on page 39).

The Molossus of the Romans (page 49) is nothing other than the big wolf-like dog still found nowadays in Albania, Montenegro and Greece; in all scientific publications regarding dogs, probably since the days of Plinius, the mistake has been made, however, of confusing the Roman Molossus with the progenitors of our Mastiffs, which were not a all related to this wolf-like dog.

6. Richard Strebel, my colleague and close friend in Germany, is in this regard of a different opinion: according to Strebel, the tendency toward albinism would be, if it were an adaptation to the snowy surroundings, much more pronounced; he believes that this form of albinism is the result of extreme incest breeding. He had the opportunity to observe this same phenomenon in a German kennel, where Fox Terriers were bred. The original color-pattern, as shown in the old pictures, was basically red with a black mask and white patches (around the year 1887). At that time it was considered to be absolutely necessary that black markings be present on the head and at the tail's point of attachment, with a fiery-red spot above each eye.

Today the best representatives of this breed are almost totally white, such as those derive from the Vesuvienne and Vesuvian lines, etc. The same phenomenon is appearing in the Bulldog.

7. Siber fails to take into account the early superstitions associated with selection of certain qualities, including color. Early reports indicate that many Tibetans believed that black and black-and-tan dogs made the best guardians. This is not unique to Tibetan dog attitudes. Early agricultural writers, Columella among them, stated that livestock guardian breeds, such as the Great Pyrenees and the Maremma-Abruzzi, were selected for their white color on the premise that this helped to distinguish them from the wolf. Other authors imply that color may indeed have been a matter of superstition and tradition. We do know that the mountain shepherds who bred the Pyrenees were a superstitious lot. They believed that dogs with double dewclaws, now an established characteristic of the breed, made the best guardians. Such an attitude was prevalent among early Beauceron breeders, too. It should be obvious that the presence or absence of dewclaws had, in reality, little effect on how well the dogs performed their work. Yet, the superstitions of their owners led to the fixing of breed traits.

Columella also advises us that many people, in the Italy of his day, who wanted guard dogs, such as the Neapolitan Mastiff, preferred black or dark-colored animals. The assumption was that these dogs would be invisible at night, thus surprising any trespasser or thief. *(Cathy J. Flamholtz)*

8. An intelligent assistant of *Livestock Journal,* London, writes in the year 1885: "It seems that animal breeds that live and have been bred over a long period of time in cold regions of high altitude are predominantly black or white in coat-color."

9. The famous St. Bernard breeder, H. Schumacher of Holligen, Switzerland, displayed stuffed anatomical representatives taxidermically prepared from young St. Bernards that had died at an early age due to a kennel infection. At the club meeting in Bern, Switzerland, in the year 1889, where he displayed them, his friends could see that they had pronounced double dewclaws on their front feet. Schumacher maintained that he had also observed Great Pyrenees with this peculiarity on several occasions. Hodgson mentioned having seen this as a breed characteristic among the Tibet Mastiffs he had seen throughout the Himalayas.

10. Charles Darwin is of a different opinion (refer to his publication *Variations in Animals and Plants,* page 20):

> "On an Assyrian monument approximately 6,400 B.C."...Darwin is probably mistaken here—possibly a misprint—with regard to the date, which should be 640 B.C....—"there is pictured a huge Mastiff, and according to Sir Henry Rawlinson, still today, as reported recently at the British Museum, similar dogs are found. I saw drawings of these dogs which were found in the grave of the son of Esar Haddon, also clay figures of these at the British Museum. They called this dog a Tibet Mastiff. Mr. H. A. Oldfield, who is an expert with regard to this dog and who checked over the drawing at the British Museum, tells me that the dog in the drawing is, in his opinion, different from a Tibet Mastiff." —We do not know, of course, exactly which drawing Darwin saw.

11. According to the Greek historian Herodotus (5th century B. C.), the ruler of Babylonia kept such a large number of dogs from India, that four large cities in the plains were not required to pay taxes as compensation for their duty and responsibility to feed and take care of his big packs of dogs. Elcazar Blaze believes that these dogs were

neither used for hunting nor for pompous shows, but were actually military dogs, "dogs of War," which belonged to Cyrus (King of Persia 550-529 B.C. and founded or the Persian Empire). However, Herodotus does not mention in any of his writings that they were "war dogs," and in our opinion, they must have been used for hunting. On the other hand, it is known that during antiquity many groups of people kept these so-called war dogs, or as the case may be, took dogs along with them on their military expeditions; indeed, the Cimbrian tribes, the Celts and the people of ancient Gaul kept dogs that were actually trained for military purposes. When the Cimbrian tribes were defeated by Marius (155-86 B.C., Roman general and consul), their encampment, which sheltered their women, children and belongings, was defended so effectively by their dogs that fresh Roman troops were necessary for their final conquest. It is also known that the ancient Swiss and Italians took dogs with them to their battles, for example, in Swiss history, Karl the Bold. Stanley reports recently that tribes in the heart of Africa near Lake Victoria keep war dogs for military purposes.

12. See Dunoyer de Noirmont's publication.

13. A note concerning the Tibet Mastiff-like dogs in Assyria was contributed by Dr. S. Birch in a publication concerning the book illustration by

Atefan ("Transactions Society of Biblical Archaeology, Vol. IV, part I, published in the year 1875), in which he pictures such a female' she resembles, according to L.S.J., more the European than the Asiatic Mastiff type. According to the decipherings of Dr. Birch, it is particularly important for us to note that this dog in the illustration is described as *Phates Kamu:* the second word here means *black* and refers to the color of the dog. From this, one of the earliest pictures, we see that among the large Mastiffs of Assyria the color *black* occurred, and that these dogs, accordingly, were similar, not only in their external appearance, but also in their color, to the present-day Tibet Mastiff.

14. Somewhat older are the reports from Ktesias, who describes the Tibet Mastiff rather correctly, but considers him to be a type of *bird.* Ktesias (416-399 B.C.) was a Greek historian and a doctor at the Persian palace in Susa. He wrote a history of Persia, from which literary fragments were preserved by Photios, Diodor and Plutarch. This information from Ktesias, according to the writings of Photios, furnishes fantastic descriptions of four-legged animals with wings *(griffins)*, which, with some modification, could still be used to portray the present-day Tibet Mastiff. In those ancient descriptions, high mountain peaks are mentioned, which were inhabited by these *griffins*, a four-

legged bird approximately the size of a wolf, with legs and claws like a lion's, but the entire body of which is covered with black feathers, which are reddish-yellow only in the chest region. As a result of these birds' watchful vigilance, Ktesias considered it extremely difficult to climb these mountains. Aelian portrays these mythical animals, using the reports by Photios, even more bird-like in his descriptions. If we, however, omit the word *bird* and substitute the word *coat* for *feathers,* we get a rather fitting description of the Tibet Mastiff, still in this form in Tibet today. These dogs are still, even now, just as in former days, the guardians of the dwellings and houses in Tibet, from where the ancient Assyrians possibly had obtained their fighting dogs. Even the black color of those mysterious animals and the red markings on their chests (breasts) coincide with the Dachshund-like colors of our present-day Tibet Mastiffs. The Tibetans call their dogs "Gyake" on account of their size and ferocity. (This information was taken from L. Beckmann's *Die Rassen des Hundes {The Breeds of the Dog}* and from information published by V. M. A. Ball of Dublin, Ireland.)

15. It has, up until now, not been possible for me to locate the original source for the reports by Megasthenes quoted by English writers.

16. Colonel Hamilton Smith, *Naturalist's Library,* 1840, page 96: "The Arcadian dogs, *Leonicii leontomiges,* said to be sprung from lions, show an approach to mastiffs, only that they were not with drooping ears; for Megasthenes, being, we believe, the most ancient writer who notices that peculiarity, would scarcely have mentioned it as such in Persia, if it had been known among any breed of dogs in Greece."

17. Idstone, *The Dog,* circa 1880, Chapter XXII, "The Mastiff," page 157: "All we know is that a race of Mastiff or Bulldog, or both, existed in this country (England) before the arrival of the Romans; and that, according to the descriptions which reach us, they were like those of Central Asia, or such as are mentioned by Megasthenes, massive of limb, muscular, broad, large-headed and with blunt muzzles."

18. This book is taken from the book entitled *Le Livre de Marco Polo (The Life of Marco Polo),* written by M. J. Pauthier and published in Paris, France, in the year 1865.

19. This information is taken from an article by Paul Wolff, which was published in the magazine *Der Hund (The Dog),* Vol. IX, pages 38 and 169. Publisher: Blasewitz of Dresden, Germany.

20. Bhutan, Bootan, Bhootan; Bhoteas, Bothes, Bhutias. Inhabitants of Bhutan, in the eastern Himalayas, eastward of Sikkim.

21. Also mentioned by Charles Darwin in his famous book *Variations...*

22. Two dogs of this breed were brought to England, where a portrait was painted of them by the famous artist Landseer, in his very typical manner of painting.

23. Gustav Kreitner's article includes, in the original publication, an illustration which shows a herd of Yaks, each carrying a load and guided by Tibetan herdsmen. Five large Tibet Mastiffs are patrolling back and forth along the rim of the herd, barking. The dogs in the illustration are somewhat low-set, massive, densely coated, with wrinkled, bulky heads and smooth-coated foreheads and muzzles; their tails are heavily coated; they seem to be flop-eared. These dogs, by the way, are only shown as indistinct figures of the background landscape.

24. These men were Seypoyas from Lahore and Peschawar.

25. In addition, Izzet Ullah, who was sent to Central Asia by Moorcraft, reports in the *Oriental*

Magazine Calcutta (January-June 1865) that the Tibet Mastiffs are twice as large as the dogs of Hindustan; they have large heads, long coats; they are very strong and courageous: indeed, it is said that they are capable of defeating a lion. (Note: taken from Pauthier or Jule: *Marco Polo.*)

26. Tibet, or "Bodyul," as the natives there refer to their country, is a large mountainous region with an altitude of 10,000 to 20,000 feet, located in the northern Himalayas, with the capital being Lhasa. Although it is the seat of Buddhism, and even though the religious and political leader, the Dalai Lama, is required to pay tribute to China, it is now (in the year 1897) actually more like a state of India, with regard to its people, as well as its plant and animal life, which are almost the same as those found in Kashmir and Nepal. The book entitled *Large Game Shooting in Tibet, the Himalayas and the Northwest* by Colonel Alexander A. Kinlock (publisher: W. Thacker & Co., London) is a larger, superbly written and illustrated sportsman's book, which renders, besides the hunting descriptions, precise information concerning the way of life, customs and economic situation in Tibet. (J. A. Petersen's book entitled *East Indian Dogs and Their Utilization as Hunting Dogs*)

27. Long-coated St. Bernards and the Newfoundland also have this soft, wooly undercoat quite frequently.

28. The dogs in Abyssinia are used in a similar manner for hunting. There they pursue the game fowl until they become tired and the dogs can catch them. (Refer to Max Siber's book *Dogs of Africa*.)

29. We observed this same phenomenon in Switzerland: Before scientific breeding was practiced in Switzerland, St. Bernards were found in a wide rang of variations as farmers' and butchers' dogs, as I can remember them during the period from 1865-1882. From these larger farmers' and butchers' dogs, the St. Bernard breed as we know it today was developed by selective breeding.

30. Siber's prediction has not proven out. Size varies greatly in the breed. In the U.S., most males average 25-28 inches, while most females average 24-26 inches. Descriptions of the size of dogs from Tibet vary widely. Some Tibetan nomads castrated their male dogs which may have resulted in artificially increased size. Different sizes of dogs may have been preferred in various areas of Tibet. The first imports to the U.S., were small or medium in size. Ann Rohrer was invited, in recent years,

to judge the breed in Taiwan. She saw very large specimens which had been imported from the sections of Tibet bordering China. No scientific study has ever been undertaken of weights within the breed. Many breeders have actively worked to breed larger dogs. Still, the weights predicted by Siber are much larger than in the dogs we see today. *(Cathy J. Flamholtz)*

31. Siber's mention of the blue color is very interesting. For years, this color was unknown to American breeders. Then, in a litter from an imported parent, this color appeared. One such blue dog was produced from Karen and Rob Pickel's breeding of the German import *Yidam Dakas Kashmir* and *Langtang Shay-Ri's Sugarfoot*. How interesting that Siber was aware of this color back in 1897. *(Cathy J. Flamholtz)*

32. Thankfully, selective breeding has all but eliminated cow-hocks and extremely straight stifles. As in any other breed, cow-hocks are considered a serious fault and cause for placing a puppy in a pet home. The Tibetan Mastiff has moderate angulation. *(Cathy J. Flamholtz)*

Bibliography

Literature-Authors

Aelian. *Hist. Anim.* p. 19, Aristotle.

Arrian. *Asiatic Researches.* 1832 and later edns.

Ausland. 1848.

Ball, V.M.A. Director of the Dublin Museum. *On the Identification of the Animals and Plants of India, Which Were Known to Early Greek Authors.* 1885.

Beckmann, Ludwig. animal artist. *Geschichte und Beschreibung der Rassen des Hundes. (History and Description of the Breeds of Dogs).* Vol. I and II. Braunschweig, Germany: Friedrich Viehweg & Sohn. ("Tibethund," Vol. II, page 86, etc.). copiously illustrated.

Bennett. *Gardens and Menagerie of the Zoological Society.* London.

Bennett, Gordon. *The Tower Menagerie.* London, 1880.

Birch, Dr. S.

Blaze, Elzéar.*Histoire du Chien. (History of the Dog)*. Paris: Croissant. 1856.

Brehm, Dr. A. *Tierleben (Animal Life)*. "Saugetiere" (Mammals), Vol. I.

Bylandt, Graf Henri. *Les Races de Chiens (The Breeds of Dogs)*. Brussels, Belgium: Vanbuggenhoudt. 1897.

Chasse et Peche, (magazine *Hunting and Fishing),* Journal *Hebdomadaire Illustré (Weekly Illustrated Journal)*. Brussels, publications I-XVI.

Chien, Le (The Dog). Paris: Chez Rothschild.

Columella.

Corsincon *see Dalziel.*

Cunningham. *Ladak.* 1854, pg. 218.

Dalziel, Hugh. *British Dogs, Their Varieties, History, Characteristics, etc., illustrated with portraits of dogs of the day.* London. pg. 275 "The Tibet Mastiff" and illustration.

Darwin, Charles. *Variations of Animals and Plants, Vol. I and II.* pgs. 35, 44, 369 and following.

Deutsche Rundschan für Geographie und Statistik (German Review of Geography and Statistics). 1880, Vol. X, pg. 341.

L'Eleveur. written on behalf of Pierre Mégnin, *Journal Hebdomadaire Illustré (Weekly Illustrated Journal).* Vincennes.

Fitzinger, Dr. Leopold. *Der Hund (The Dog).* Vienna, Austria.

Fraser, J.B.

Gayot, Eugene. *Le Chien (The Dog)*. Paris: Firmin Didot.1867. Figure 73, "Le Mastiff de Tibet."

Gill. *The River of Golden Sand.*

Gratius Faliscus. *Carmen Venaticum (Song of the Chase).* around 159 BC.

Hamilton Smith, Lieutenant-Colonel. *Naturalist's Library,* Vol. X, "Mammalia, Dogs." Edinburgh: W. H. Lizarz. 1840.

Henderson and Hume. *From Lahor to Yarkand.* 1873. pg. 61.

Herodotus. *Musæ.*

Hodgson, Bryan. *Drawing of Nepalese Animals.* 1830.

Hooker, Dr. *Himalayan Journals.* London. 1854.

Hosie. *Three Years in Western China.* 1890, p. 134.

Hund, Der. periodical *(The Dog)* Vol. I-XIV. Dresden, Germany: Paul Wolff, Blazewitz.

Bertram, C.A. Windle & John Humphrey. "On Some Cranial and Dental Characteristics of the Domestic Dog," *Proc. Zool. Soc.,* 1880 (contains information regarding the Tibet Mastiff's skull).

Idstone. *The Dog.* London: Cassel, Peter, Galpin & Co. 6th edn. 1880. p. 156, "The Mastiff."

Illustrated London News.

Journal Asiatic. Vol. IX, p. 218.1826.

Journal Asiatic Society of Bengal. Vol. I, pg. 342. 1832.

Journal Geographic Society. London.

"Katalog der Gruppe 45" ("Catalog of Group 45"), *Jagd und Fischere (Hunting and Fishing* magazine). Geneva, Switzerland. National dog show. 1896.

Kinlock, Colonel Alexander. *Large Game Shooting in Tibet, the Himalayas and the Northwest.* London: Thacker, Spinck & Co.

Kreitner, Gustav. *Im fernen Osten (In the Far East).* Vienna. 1881.

Krichler, Franz. *Zentralblatt für Jagd- und Hunde-Liebhaber (Central Journal for Hunting and Dog Enthusiasts).* St. Gallen, Switzerland. 1892.

Ktesias.

Langkavel, Dr. Bernhard, of Hamburg.

Layard. *Babylon.*

Leipziger Illustrierte Zeitung (Illustrated Newspaper of Leipzig, Germany). 1892-1893.

Livestock Journal. London. Vols. from 1880-1887.

Marco Polo.

Markham. *Narrative of the Mission of G. A. Bogle.* pgs. 68 and 116.

Martin, W.C.L. *The History of the Dog, its Origin, Physical and Moral Characteristics and its Principal Varieties.* London. 1845.

Megasthenes.

Mégnin, Pierre. *Les Races de Chiens (The Breeds of Dogs).* Vincennes. 3rd and 4th editions. 1890 and 1896.

Merk, J. N.

Moorcroft. *Reise nach dem Manasa-Sarovara-See (Trip to the Manasa-Sarovara-Lake)*, in English translation *Travels in Himalayan Provinces*. Vol. I, pg. 309. 1841.

Mortillet, Gabriel de. *Origines de la Chasse, de la Pêche et de l'Agriculture (Origins of Hunting, Fishing and Agriculture)*. Vol. I. Paris. 1890.

Moss-King, Mrs. Robert. *Die Frau eines Civilbeamten in Indien (The Wife of a Government Official in India)*.

Müller, Johannes von. *Schweizer-geschichte (Swiss History)*.

Nehring, Professor, from Berlin.

Neue Deutsche Jagdzeitung (New German Hunting Magazine). Vol. I-XIV. Paul Baensch, publisher.

Nott and Giddon. *Types of Mankind*.

Noirmont, Dunoyer de. *Le Baron (The Baron)*. Paris: Bouchard-Huzard. 1868.

Österreichisches Kynologisches Jahrbuch (Austrian Canine Science Annual). Vienna: Paul Gerin. Vol. I. 1897.

Oriental Magazine. Calcutta, India.

Pauthier, M. G. *Le Livre de Marco Polo (The Life of Marco Polo)*. Paris: Firmin Didot. 1865.

Petermann's Geographische Mittheilungen (Pertermann's Geographical Information). 1883 and 1891. pg. 347 and pg. 222.

Peterson, J. A. *Uber Ostindische Hunde und ihre Verwendung zur Jagd (About East Indian Dogs and their Utlization for Hunting).* St. Gallen, Switzerland: Zollikofer. 1895.

Photios.

Plinius. *Hist. nat.*

Prschewalkski, N. von. *Reisen in Tibet (Travels in Tibet).* Jena, Germany. pg. 180 and 276.

Radde, Gustav. *Kaukasus (Caucasus Mountains).*

Rapes, Captain. *Expedition zur Entdeckung der Ganges-Quellen (Expedition for the Discovery of the Ganges River Origins).* 1846.

Reichenbach, Dr. H. G. *Der Hund in seinen Haupt- und Nebenrassen. (The Dog in His Main and Subsidiary Breeds).* Leipzig, Germany. 1836.

Reul, Adolph. *Les Races de Chiens (The Breeds of Dogs).* Brussels, Belgium. 1891-1894.

Révoil. *Historique des Chiens (History of Dogs).* Paris.

Robert, Jean. *Le Chien d'appartement et d'utilité. (The Companion and Working Dog).* Paris.

Rockhill. *The Land of the Lamas.* pgs. 139 and 367. 1891.

Rütimeyer, Dr. Professor L. *Die Fauna der Pfahlbauten. (The Fauna {Animals} of the Lake Dwellers).* 1868.

Schlagintweit, v. *Reisen. (Travels).* Vol. III, pg. 280 and following.

Schweizerisches Hunde-Stammbuch. (Swiss Dog Registry Book). St. Gallen, Switzerland: Zollikofer and Zurich, Switzerland: A. Müller. Vols. II-VII (1887-1893).

Schumacher, H. from Hollingen, near Bern, Switzerland.

Shaw, Vero. *The Illustrated Book of the Dog.* London.

Siber, Max. *Hunde Afrikas. (Dogs of Africa).* St. Gallen, Switzerland: Zollikofer.

Siegmund, Benjamin. *Schweizerisches Hunde-Stammbach. (Swiss Dog Registry Book).* Basel, Switzerland: Grossrath. Vols. II, III, and V.

Solinus. pg. 15.

Stables, Gordon. *The Dog.* London.

Stanley. *Through the Dark Continent.*

Stonehenge. *The Dog.* London.

Strabon's Erdbeschreibung. (Strabon's Description of the Earth). by G. Groskurd. Berlin. 1831.

Strebel, Richard. artist. Munich, Germany.

Studer, Professor Theodor. writing in *Swiss Dog Registry Book,* Vol I and others.

Sundeval, Carl J. *Die Thierarten des Aristoteles. (The Animal Species of Aristotle).* Stockholm, Sweden. 1863.

The Tower Menagerie. London. 1829. illustrated by William Harvey.

Transactions of the Society of Biblical Archaeology. 1875.

Turner, Captain. *Account of an Embassy to the Court of the Teshoo Lama in Tibet.* 1800.

Turner, Samuel. *Gesandschaftsreise durch Bhootan nach Tibet. (Envoy Trip through Bhutan to Tibet).* Hamburg. 1801.

Ujfalvy, K. Eugen. *Aus dem Westlichen Himalaya. (From the Western Himalayas).* Leipzig, Germany. 1884.

Walter, Dr. C.F.H. *Der Hund nach Youatt. (The Dogs Described by Youatt).* Stuttgart, Germany. 1852.

Youatt. *The Dog.* London.

Yule, Colonel. *The Book of Marco Polo.* Vol. II, pg. 33. London. 1871.

Zentralblatt für Jagd-und Hundeliebhaber. (Central Journal for Hunters and Dog Enthusiasts). Vol. I-IX. St. Gallen, Switzerland: Zollikofer.

OTHER FINE BOOKS FROM OTR

A Celebration of Rare Breeds, Volumes I and II
by Cathy J. Flamholtz

America's most popular books on rare breeds. Both nominated for top honors by the Dog Writers' Association of America. Volume I covers 53 breeds (including the Tibetan Mastiff), some of which have since gained AKC recognition. Volume II covers an additional 35 breeds, including some in the AKC line-up. Find out why the critics rave.

Volume I $24.95 + $2.50 p&h   Volume II $27.95 + $2.50 p&h

The Tibetan Mastiff
by Ann Rohrer & Cathy J. Flamholtz

"...this is a great read. Peruse the TM volume as a travel/adventure tale crammed with exotic information...It is reminiscent of the memoirs of...19th century explorers of mysterious lands. Rohrer is a keen observer whose eye takes in far more than the bearlike TM. Ms. Flamholtz, whose able pen and elegant style are apparent throughout, adds much to the joy of following the breed's saga...This book is a treasure. Read and enjoy." Deborah Lawson, *Dog News* $16.95 + $2.50 p&h

Livestock Protection Dogs
Selection, Care and Training
by David E. Sims, PhD & Orysia Dawydiak

Selected *Best Care and Training Book of the Year* by the Dog Writers' Association of America, this highly acclaimed paperback, which includes the Tibetan Mastiff, has earned praise from breeders and ranchers alike. This complete guide tells you all you need to know, from the moment the puppy arrives to the care and management of the adult. Includes a revolutionary chapter on temperament testing these dogs. $9.95 + $2.00 p&h

The Working Airedale
by Bryan Cummins, PhD

Dr. Cummins has penned a landmark work on the historical and contemporary uses of the King of Terriers. A true testament to the largest member of the terrier clan, you won't want to miss this unique book. $24.95 + $2.50 p&h

See the next page for additional titles and ordering information.